The Golden Age of Italian Jews

The Golden Age of Italian Jews

1848–1938

Gino Segrè

pdb

PAUL DRY BOOKS

Philadelphia 2025

First Paul Dry Books Edition, 2025
Second printing

Paul Dry Books, Inc.
Philadelphia, Pennsylvania
www.pauldrybooks.com

Printed in the United States of America

Map by Robert Cronan of Lucidity Information Design, LLC.

Library of Congress Control Number: 2025936164
ISBN: 978-1-58988-205-8

To the memory of my grandmother
Amelia Treves Segrè (1864-1943)

Contents

Timeline

B.C.E.

161	Jewish delegation arrives in Rome
45	Death of Julius Caesar

C.E.

70	Destruction of Jerusalem's Second Temple
313	Emperor Constantine favors Christianity
756	Foundation of Papal State
800	Charlemagne is crowned as Holy Roman Emperor
1492	Alhambra Decree: Jews expelled from Spain
1515	First ghetto established in Venice
1555	Paul IV becomes pope: Rome's ghetto created
1782	Joseph II, Holy Roman Emperor, Issues Edict of Toleration
1796	First foray of Napoleon into Italy
1848	Statuto Albertino—Kingdom of Sardinia' Constitution
1861	Proclamation of Kingdom of Italy
1866	Venice becomes part of Kingdom of Italy
1870	Italian troops conquer Rome—Pope Pius IX retreats to Vatican
1878	Death of King Victor Emanuel II and of Pope Pius IX
1900	Assassination of King Umberto I
1915	Italy enters WWI

1918	End of WWI
1922	March on Rome-Mussolini becomes Italy's prime minister
1925	Italy become dictatorship under Mussolini
1935	Italy declares war on Ethiopia
1936	Spanish Civil War begins
1938	Racial Laws passed in Italy
1939	Beginning of WWII
1943	Italy surrenders to Allies and Germans occupy Italy
1945	End of WWII

The Golden Age of Italian Jews

Italy in 1848

Prologue

THE PERIOD from 1848 to 1938 was a golden age for Italian Jews. Almost a century long, this era stretches from when Jews in much of nascent Italy were finally given full civil rights until when they were denied those same rights throughout a country that was drawing closer to Nazi Germany. Over that time, they made great contributions to their country's evolution from backward, divided, and agrarian into a united powerful nation. The impact of Jews was completely out of proportion to their numbers, which were never more than a tenth of one percent of Italy's total population. By World War I, Italian Jews had risen to positions of power and prestige that were severely restricted or closed to Jews elsewhere in Europe. Compared to the Jewish population of France, a neighboring country of similar size but with far more Jews, the Jews of Italy were considerably more prominent.

It was an era in which Jewish generals and admirals were an integral part of Italy's armed forces; Rome had a Jewish mayor; Italy a Jewish prime minister; and Jews held more than six percent of the country's university professorships. These positions, unthinkable for Jews before 1848, were blocked after 1938.

Many questions spring to mind. How did they, this small assemblage of individuals, one in a thousand of the country's total population, manage to become so successful? What was it in their background that made this possible? In what ways was the country's earlier history important? What role had the papacy played in the past, and what role did it play during the golden era? Was leaving the ghetto a form of emigration, albeit an internal one?

This book explores both how and why this golden age

occurred. As a scientist, I seek clear answers. As an amateur historian, I long for illuminating trends. As an Italian Jew, I hope for a better understanding of this piece of my life. As an author of several books, I struggle with how to tell this story. The book weaves a journey through this century-long era of Italian history by combining lives of individuals, including family members of mine, with the external factors that first helped and then hindered the processes of acceptance and assimilation.

In the mid-nineteenth century, once restrictions on the entry of Jews into Italian society were lifted, it was relatively easy for them to fit in; Jews spoke, dressed, and looked like other Italian citizens. They had no language of their own, such as Yiddish. In assimilating, they frequently even stopped being observant. Abandoning those tenets would not have been possible earlier, when Italian Jews were confined within ghettos and lived perforce in tightly knit communities. Threatened by outsiders and by arbitrary rules, they survived by uniting around common mores. But all that changed with the disappearance of ghetto walls.

It then became commonplace to see Italian Jews abandoning the deep faith that had governed their ancestors' lives. A cousin of my father's, born like him in 1891, wrote late in her life about the shifts that she had witnessed.

> Faith, for the old ones, was comfort, union, sustenance, and it filled every hour of the day. They had absorbed it in their youth like the very air, and their whole lives had been filled by it, but in a world round them that had changed, they had not been able to teach it, even to their children.

Yet for the most part Italian Jews quietly retained their Jewish cultural identity as a private matter, even when they stopped being observant, and even when, as my father did, they partnered with individuals of other faiths. Perhaps that enduring identity was due to the shared history of centuries of oppression, memories of which were horribly reawakened in 1938. The golden age died then, and its horrid aftermath came five years later when Nazi forces occupied much of Italy and brought a tragic end to those they captured who could be identified as Jewish. This is where the book begins.

CHAPTER 1

October 1943

IN OCTOBER 1943 the golden age that Italian Jews had been enjoying for nearly a century ended abruptly with the passage of laws stigmatizing them and inhibiting the roles they could play in society. Life quickly became very difficult, and then even threatened.

On July 10, 1943, combined British and American troops landed in Sicily, prompting the Italian Government to depose Mussolini and replace him with the seventy-two-year -old Marshal Pietro Badoglio, the chief of staff of the Italian Army. The first step toward negotiating a surrender took place on September 8. The new government quickly repealed the Racial Laws passed in the fall of 1938, but this did little good because Germany then sent its troops into Italy. They turned the country north of Naples into a virtual German protectorate. A puppet republican government was set up in Salò, a tranquil town in northern Italy that lay on the shores of the beautiful Lake Garda. This new regime was headed by Mussolini, but control of it was kept firmly in German hands.

Most Italian Jews were alarmed, fearing the Germans intended to make them part of Hitler's Final Solution. Those who had fled the country in preceding years were safe, but they were the exception. My uncle Emilio and my father, Angelo, were two of them. They had found it easier to leave Italy because both were married to German women; their wives had no extended Italian family ties and no historic loyalty to Italy. It was also the case that the brothers, having themselves spent long periods of time in Germany and having friends and family contacts there through their wives, were more aware of what might soon happen. They both emigrated to the United States with their families; Emilio in 1938 and my father the following year.

Angelo and Emilio encouraged their parents, who had supported their departures, to come to the United States, or at least consider emigrating to Argentina, a country whose Latin atmosphere might feel more comfortable to them, and where they also had relatives. But their father thought that, while his two sons, as academics, could start their careers over again, he was simply too old. He did, however, let them know that he would take precautions to protect himself and their mother in case matters got worse in Italy. Emilio remembered the last words his father said to him: "You are right in going. If I were a half-century younger, I would do the same."

Marco, the third brother, did consider emigrating to Argentina, but in the end rejected doing so. His Italian wife was reluctant to make the move, and he was also held back by his close involvement in the operation of the family paper mill.

Italian Jews had known life would be difficult after the passage of the Racial Laws, but they trusted in the acceptance Italy had shown them in the previous decades. Some even believed the discriminatory decrees might not be long-lived. The German occupation that began in 1943 meant they needed to consider their options.

The first month of having German soldiers in their midst passed relatively quietly. There were sporadic roundups of small numbers of Jews in Northern Italy, but nothing of the sort took place in Rome, the Italian city with the largest Jewish population. Hoping the occupation was only temporary, but still apprehensive, many Jews went into hiding, often with fake identity documents. My uncle Marco and his family took this route, while my grandparents arranged to be sheltered in a nearby Catholic convent should they need to hide and find protection.

Hans Kappler, the newly appointed German head of police and security in Rome, told the city's Jewish community that its registered members would not be harmed, and extorted from them a payment of fifty kilograms of gold as a guarantee for their safety. He did not reveal that a SS unit of fourteen officers and thirty soldiers had already been dispatched from Berlin to Rome; they were a group specially trained to assist German soldiers already in place in implementing the Final Solution. When they arrived, Kappler gave them a list of all known Roman Jews and their residences. He also assigned three hundred of the troops under his command to help carry out their upcoming task.

The roundup on the Sabbath, Saturday, October 16, came as a complete surprise to Rome's Jews. At 5:30 in the morning two hundred German soldiers closed off the old ghetto and began going door to door. The ghetto as such no longer existed, but many of Rome's Jews, particularly the poor, continued to live in that section of the city. Those captured were taken to a nearby military academy and locked into its courtyard. Meanwhile, other German soldiers deployed throughout the rest of the city to seek its Jews.

My grandparents were on the list of those to be apprehended. An acquaintance, an Italian employee of the German, saw the list and telephoned them, alerting my grandparents to their danger. My grandfather immediately called his chauffeur to bring them to their planned refuge and, with my grandmother, left from their second-floor apartment to go down to the waiting car. As they were about to enter the car, my grandmother remembered she had forgotten her jewelry and went back, saying she would return right away.

It was a fatal mistake. A minute after she left the car, a truck with German soldiers drove up to the entrance of the apartment building and marched in. The panicked chauffeur drove away with my grandfather. He knew that intervening would have meant both of them would be arrested. That was the last time

AMELIA TREVES SEGRÈ—MY GRANDMOTHER

my grandfather saw my seventy-nine-year-old grandmother; he tried to get information of her whereabouts but there was none. Heartbroken, he died soon afterwards of natural causes.

Arriving in the courtyard of the military academy where she would be confined with the Jews rounded up earlier in the day, my grandmother must have looked around for a familiar face. Most of the Jews surrounding her were unfamiliar to her, but I like to think she saw Augusto Capon; he was someone from her own social circle, and that might have given her some comfort. When apprehended, Capon, an admiral of the Italian navy, had been wearing his full military uniform with all his badges pinned to his chest. He was hard to miss. She knew that his daughter was married to Enrico Fermi, arguably Italy's greatest scientist since Galileo. Fermi was not Jewish, but since his wife was, his children were as well, according to Racial Laws. Fortunately, they had all left Italy for the United States in 1938. The Admiral knew my grandmother, too, because in 1927 her son Emilio had become Fermi's first student, and they had worked together for the following decade. Whether or not my grandmother connected with Capon that day is still unknown.

Eighty years old and semi-paralyzed from a stroke, Admiral Capon had refused to go into hiding when Fermi's sister Maria, still in Rome, offered to hide him in her apartment. On October 16, alerted of the roundup, he changed into his full military regalia. When the German soldiers arrived at his villa, he showed them a warm personal letter written to him by Mussolini, expecting the soldiers to acknowledge its content, recognize his rank, and leave. Instead, they ignored the letter, dragged him to the truck parked outside, and threw him in it.

After two days in the courtyard of the military academy, the captured Jews were taken to the railroad station and loaded into sealed windowless boxcars. The journey north then began. It made no stops for food or drink. Four days later, the Jews arrived at Auschwitz. Descending from the boxcars, the passengers were separated into two groups. The young, fit, and strong, intended for hard labor, were directed to the right. The others, an overwhelming majority, were sent to the left, supposedly for showers, but instead they were sent to gas chambers. There were 1,020 Jews in the convoy. Only sixteen survived; fifteen men and one woman. After the war, one of those survivors recounted having been in the same boxcar as Admiral Capon and having heard him say to the others trapped with him, "We are going toward our death. You don't know the Germans. I fought against them in World War I." Nobody wanted to believe him.

CHAPTER 2

All Families Are Not Alike

HIDDEN AWAY in a Roman countryside retreat, my uncle Marco quickly learned that all the Roman Jews the German soldiers could find had been rounded up and taken away. He also discovered that his father was safe but his mother was not. Having no further news of her fate, he feared the worst. He wanted to tell his two brothers, safely living in America, what had happened, but there was an embargo on mail because German-occupied Italy was at war with the Allies.

My uncle Emilio found out anyway. At the time, he was in the secret city of Los Alamos, one of three senior Italian physicists working on the Manhattan Project, whose primary mission was building an atomic bomb before the Germans did. The project's director, J. Robert Oppenheimer, was alerted by reports that had reached Washington and told to inform Emilio that his mother had been abducted and was in Nazi hands. Emilio was stunned. Oppenheimer, thinking Emilio had not understood what he had just said, repeated the message several times.

Emilio also wondered if the father of Fermi's wife Laura had been caught in the roundup. Fermi was working elsewhere on the Manhattan Project, and his family had not yet moved to Los Alamos. When they did, Emilio and Laura conferred frequently but no news was forthcoming.

I am unaware of how my father learned what happened in Rome that October of 1943. I imagine Uncle Emilio contacted him. He never spoke about it. In fact, he never shared with me anything about his parents or his childhood. All I know of his early life is what I have read in letters, books, or was told by my mother and relatives. He seemed to have put his early family history in a sealed box. My mother later told me that after his mother's disappearance my father began suffering from insomnia and nightmares. As a child, I knew that something was wrong since, bleary-eyed in the morning, he frequently complained, of *sognacci* (bad dreams) during the night, but I didn't know the cause or their content.

I believe he felt he had failed his parents yet again. Feelings of this kind had begun early in his life. His domineering father, a successful, self-made industrialist, intended that my father, Angelo, the first-born, would run the thriving paper mill he had built in Tivoli, a beautiful hill town near Rome. Angelo, a sensitive and difficult child, disappointed him. Not only did he not display a temperament suitable for an industrialist, but he was also far more interested in the nearby ruins of ancient Rome than in the modern paper mill. He tried to fit into his expected career by enrolling for a university engineering degree but soon abandoned the program. He then joined the army but was put on home leave because of a bad case of pleurisy, only to be enrolled again during World War I. Assigned at that time to a military intelligence unit, he did not see action at the front. Since he continued to show little interest in the paper mill, his father finally decided that Angelo's two-years-younger brother, Marco, should be the one to carry on the family legacy; Marco was more than happy to oblige.

Intent on completing a university program but finding life in Rome stressful, Angelo decamped to Parma where his uncle Gino was a distinguished law professor with a specialty in Roman Law. With his early interest in antiquity rekindled, Angelo finished his degree and began contemplating an academic career, but he first went off for three years of research at the universities of Vienna and Munich, both renowned as centers of scholarship related to the ancient classical world. Further studies was the given reason for his departure, but he was also eager to leave Italy behind for a while.

Troubled by Angelo's errant behavior, his parents thought marriage might stabilize him but realized his unsteadiness would make it hard to find a match for him in their circles. They were surprised and somewhat shocked when he returned to Italy from his stay in Northern Europe accompanied by Katia, a beautiful twenty-three-year-old aspiring artist. She was a German Catholic from a proletarian family, not exactly what his parents or his relatives expected.

Katia was the oldest of six children whose mother had died when she was only nine years old. At the beginning of World War I, Katia was compelled to leave school to work in a munition's factory: she was fourteen. Four years later, the war over, she left her birthplace of Cologne for Munich with a dream of becoming an artist. That was where, a few years later, she met my father. He asked her to go back to Florence with him. Having already survived poverty, near starvation during the war, and later both influenza and tuberculosis, she decided why not take a chance and do so. Though she was not welcomed into the extended Segrè family, her optimism and joie de vivre was exactly what my father needed, and the young couple fit into a quasi-Bohemian Florentine life. Several years later—once the family's reluctance to accept Katia was a thing of the past—she and my father married.

A good deal of what I know about the Segrè brothers' early life comes from an autobiography my uncle Emilio wrote in his later years. *A Mind Always in Motion*, written in 1985, is a document of a certain genre: distinguished scientists writing their memoirs. Winning the 1959 Physics Nobel Prize qualified Emilio for membership in this group. It is an exceptionally frank book, not unexpectedly, since my uncle was never known for trying to be amiable. In his younger days, when the small group of physicists working with Fermi took nicknames, his was *Il Basilisco*—a Basilisk being a legendary fire-spitting monster. In the book's sections about Italy, he expresses his admiration of his father, his enormous regard for Fermi, and his dislike

KATIA AND ANGELO AT THE TIME THEY MET

of his brother Marco, who he felt tried to alienate him from his parents. He also recounts his ongoing difficulties with my father. It is clear that World War II tore the family apart and the three brothers never managed to reconcile their differences.

I got to know Emilio well after I became a physicist, when I spent two years (1965-1967) as a postdoctoral fellow in Berkeley, where Emilio was a well-established physics professor. However, we spoke very little about family matters and nothing at all about the events of October 1943. Even in his autobiography, all Emilio wrote was "The tragic and painful page of my parents' end is buried in the depths of my soul and must remain there."

Reading that autobiography was revealing, but its one-line preface later pointed me in a different direction. It is a quote from Dante's *Divine Comedy*, in Canto X of the poet's journey through Inferno. Dante is addressed by a condemned spirit, Farinata degli Uberti, who is being punished for his heretic denial of the soul's immortality by being entombed from the waist down. Rising from his grave, the sinner asks Dante

"*Chi fuor li maggior tui*," loosely translated as "Who were your ancestors?"

Trying to answer the question "who were the *maggior* of my father and his brothers?" has led me to ask what it meant for them to be Jewish, and, more broadly, what has it meant through time to be an Italian Jew? Due to Italy's central location in South-Central Europe and its complicated history, its Jews are probably as much or more a mixture of Sephardic, Ashkenazim, and Mizrahi than in any other country in Europe, and their roots and ways of worshiping once differed greatly, each group initially building in Italy its own sub-community and its own synagogue.

It is also hard to separate the identity forged by Italian Jews from national identity because prior to the mid-nineteenth century, Italy was a collection of duchies, principalities, and regions governed by foreign powers. Moreover, a vast swath of land ruled by the pope lay at its center. The proclamation of Italy as a nation did not take place until 1861 and its annexation of Rome only occurred in 1870. The country's Jews had to forge not only a common Jewish identity but a common national one as well.

What did this history mean for my father, himself a professor of ancient history? He learned to read many ancient languages, but there is one that he never fully mastered: Hebrew. Neither he nor his brothers were bar mitzvah, and they did not go to synagogue. His brothers at least maintained some continuity with their *maggior* by marrying Jewish women and doing so in a synagogue, but he did not.

There was an extra irony in my father's separation from his roots. His deeply religious grandfather had been the architect of Florence's grand synagogue, but despite spending much of his adult life in Florence, Angelo remained estranged from that part of his family and stayed away from the synagogue.

This left my mother, my brother, and me with a problem when he passed away. He had suffered from heart disease for many years, but he did not want to speak of dying and certainly not of where he should be buried. But after he died, the problem had to be faced. The answer seemed clear to us: with his *maggior.* We contacted cousins who were prominent members of Florence's Jewish community, enrolled my father in the community, and laid him to rest in the Jewish cemetery that his grandfather had designed. We hope he would have been at peace with the arrangement.

GRAVESTONE OF MY FATHER, ANGELO SEGRÈ.
PHOTO COURTESY OF THE AUTHOR.

CHAPTER 3

2000 Years of Jewish Rome

MIGRATION brought Jews to Italy from Spain, Portugal, Northern France, Germany's Rhineland, and from elsewhere in the Mediterranean during the fourteenth, fifteenth, and sixteenth centuries. But there was a group of Jews that had already been living in Rome for centuries, having arrived there even before the Christian era, some even settling there when it was still a republic. Direct descendants of those Jews still reside in the city, making them one of the world's oldest continuous communities. Tracing the lineage of any individual that far back is a daunting task, though it may be possible with modern genetic tools. The record of those times and the memory of the successes and of the sufferings endured in Rome over the millennia is a crucial part of Italian Judaism's history.

Jews were strongly supported by Julius Caesar. Suetonius, the Roman historian who chronicled the life of the Caesars, describes Jews tearfully attending Caesar's funeral. At the height of Rome's grandeur as an Empire there may have been as many as thirty thousand Jews living in the city, out of its total population of a million. Some were slaves, but others were successful merchants.

The history of Jews under the Roman Empire is, however, best known for the destruction of the Second Temple in Jerusalem, the great tragedy that befell Jews in 70 C.E. Roman troops commanded by Titus, son of an emperor and later one himself, had laid siege to the city four years earlier. The Roman Empire embraced many cultures, and Judaism was only one of the numerous religions that were tolerated to some measure within its boundaries. The siege was simply a question of putting down a rebellious territory, a military rather than a religious mission, but the defeat was an existential crisis for the Jews because the Second Temple had been their central gathering place for centuries. It was where religious observances were held and sacrifices were made. Its destruction put an end to the dream of a Judea under Jewish control. Many Jews were killed during the Romans' four-year siege, and almost a thousand of those who survived were brought in chains to Rome as slaves.

A grand triumphal arch was raised in Rome to commemorate Titus's victory. Its symbolic importance was inescapable, for the massive bas-relief at the top of the Arch of Titus depicts vanquished Jews in chains and shows troops carrying away loot, including a giant menorah. The sixteenth-century Counter-Reformation pope, Paul IV, emphasized the message of the arch by making Rome's Jews swear loyalty to him while facing it. In return, Jews quietly made a historic promise to never walk through the arch until they held the ancient land of Palestine. They had to wait hundreds of years for that to occur. On the evening of December 2, 1947, the first Sabbath after the General Assembly of the United Nations passed the resolution partitioning Palestine into Jewish and Arab states, Rome's Chief Rabbi gathered more than a thousand of his followers at the arch and they slowly began to file through it.

Christianity in the Roman Empire was persecuted to a certain extent but eventually fully accepted, as witnessed by the early-fourth-century conversion of the Emperor Constantine. However, Christianity did not regard Judaism as simply another religion and it felt the need to clarify that divergence. The Old Testament was sacred to both Jews and Christians; worshippers of other faiths could be seen as having been led astray by misguided notions, but Jews were the descendants of ones who had been led to the Messiah, the Son of God, but had refused to recognize his divinity. This rejection made Judaism more than simply another religion.

As Rome became more Christian, it was also coming under attack by tribes from the north, so-called barbarians. Under pressure, the Empire split into two halves. In the year 402, the capital of the western half was moved to Ravenna, a city on the Adriatic coast that was thought to be easier to defend. Meanwhile Rome, in serious decline and no longer the center of an empire, came to be effectively ruled by the city's archbishop, the pope. This precarious situation lasted until the late eighth century when Charlemagne came to power. Succeeding in uniting under his aegis much of western and central Europe, he was crowned Holy Roman Emperor by Pope Leo II on Christmas day of the year 800.

However, Rome itself, and a large swath of central Italy that centered on the city were not under Charlemagne's control. His father had donated the land to the pope, thus marking the birth of a Papal State. From then on, and for more than a thousand years, whoever was pope would be a political force to be reckoned with in Italy, as well as a spiritu`al guide to Catholics everywhere. This would have profound effects on the history of Italian Jews, many of whom now found themselves directly under the rule of the Catholic Church.

Rome's Jews were at first treated relatively benignly, in that there were no pogroms like the twelfth-century ones in London and York. On the other hand, conditions depended largely on who was pope at the time. The cultural illumination engendered by the Renaissance and the increased worldliness of the popes gradually led to a more benevolent attitude toward Rome's Jews, so much so that the last decades of the fifteenth century and the first of the sixteenth have sometimes been referred to as their first golden age.

A spirit of openness toward new worlds was flourishing, and a growing interest in antiquity's documents was leading scholars to venture into new territory. Hebrew began to be added to Latin and Greek as a third language required for a full understanding of the past. Jews mixed in every aspect of society; openness and tolerance marked this golden age and their numbers swelled.

That acceptance of Jews was short lived. By the middle of the sixteenth century, other winds were blowing. Spain and Portugal had expelled their Jews, and the parts of Southern Italy under Spanish control were following suit. That didn't challenge Catholic Church doctrine, but the growth of Protestantism in Northern Europe did, and the Church felt it needed to take action to protect its primacy. A move known as the Counter Reformation began to take place.

On the 23rd of May, 1555, seventy-nine-year-old Cardinal Gian Pietro Carafa was chosen as pope. Taking the name Paul IV, this austere, rigid doctrinaire was known for having persuaded an earlier pope to introduce the Inquisition to Rome, modeling it on its Spanish counterpart. Paul IV was also reported to have once said that if his own father was a heretic, he would gather the wood to burn him.

In mid-July of 1555, less than two months after being chosen, Paul IV made his views about Jews known by issuing the notorious papal bull *Cum nimis absurdum*. Its first sentence set the tone. "Since it is completely senseless and inappropriate to be in a situation where Christian piety allows the Jews (whose guilt—all of their own doing—has condemned them to eternal slavery) access to our society and even to live among us; indeed, they are without gratitude to Christians."

Paul IV used this as a rationale to create a ghetto in Rome. During previous centuries Jews had often been obliged to live in a certain section of the city, but a ghetto was something new. Started as an institution in Venice less than forty years earlier, it was essentially an open-air prison, enclosed by walls or other natural boundaries. In the case of Venice, the boundary was a canal surrounding a small island. Guards stationed at the entrances enforced rules determining when Jews were allowed to circulate in the city—usually from dawn to dusk. Jews were also obliged to wear an identifying mark such as a yellow star when they left the ghetto.

Paul IV chose to build Rome's ghetto in the area adjacent to the Tiber River, where frequent flooding made it subject to outbreaks of cholera. The conditions Jews faced there were unhealthy as well as restrictive, intentionally degrading. Taxed heavily, they were not able to own property or engage in any but menial activities. Only a few decades earlier, Jews had been the city's elite doctors, even tending to the health of the pope. Now they were rag-pickers or menders of used clothing they sold to Romans who could afford nothing better.

Paul IV not only made Jews swear loyalty to him in front of the Arch of Titus; he also required them to congregate on the Sabbath just outside the ghetto, in front of the Church of San Gregorio and listen to Catholic sermons chastising them for failing to recognize the true God. Legend has it that many secretly put wax in their ears before attending.

Demeaning displays were obligatory on Roman holidays. The traditional first race at Carnival time featured Jews running semi-naked while spectators pelted them with mud. Another annual humiliating ritual was Rome's Chief Rabbi asking the city council permission for his brethren to live within the ghetto. It would be granted in a ceremony marked at its conclusion by his receiving a kick in the rear.

Extending their reach throughout the peninsula, Paul IV and successive popes decreed that all Italian cities with sizeable populations establish ghettos. By the late 1700s, three quarters of Italian Jews were living in the forty-one ghettos that had been created. Those in towns too small to have a ghetto were frequently ordered to move to the nearest city that had one. Conditions in them varied, but Rome's was reported to be the worst. It would also become Europe's last to be abolished.

CHAPTER 4

The Comings and Goings of Italian Jews

THE COMMON belief that Italy's Jews were primarily Sephardim fleeing the Iberian Peninsula is easily dispelled by the long history of Roman Jews and by arrivals in Italy of additional Jews from Northern Europe. But the truth is even more complicated. During approximately the same period when Jews began coming to Rome, other Jewish settlements were appearing throughout the Mediterranean. Greece and Egypt were favorite choices, and Sicily, that Italian island crossroad in the Mediterranean, was another prime location. It continued to be a relatively welcoming option for Jews even when, like Spain, it was under Muslim rule.

By the middle of the fifteenth century more Jews lived in the Kingdom of Sicily than in all the rest of what we now call Italy, their number on the island rising to 25,000. But by then, that kingdom had also become a vassal of the Spanish crown, so its Jews suffered the same 1492 expulsion their Spanish brethren endured.

Sicilian Jews then dispersed throughout the Mediterranean. Salonica and Izmir were popular destinations. Those who chose to stay on Italian soil moved north into the adjoining Kingdom of Naples, but their stay there was relatively brief, for Naples too came under Spanish control forty years later. Expelled once again, the Jews continued north, settling in the Papal State or beyond. They blended there with Sephardim expelled from Spain or Portugal, Ashkenazim from Northern Europe, and a smattering of Mizrahi from Northern Africa. Sixteenth-century Italy became a veritable Jewish melting pot.

By the beginning of the seventeenth century, most Italian Jews lived in ghettos. With different origins, ghetto dwellers at first mixed only tentatively. Venice was a perfect example. The ghetto, located on Venice's lagoon, had five separate synagogues. The German synagogue was inaugurated in 1528, the French one in 1531, the Levantine (Middle Eastern) one in 1538, the Spanish one in 1555, and the Italian one in 1575. Each had a somewhat different service and its own Jewish subcommunity in attendance. The same was true in cities like Mantua or Ferrara, smaller and less visible than Venice, but still at the crossroads of Jewish settlements.

Jews who had settled in small communities of the Papal State were forced to move again after Pope Paul IV's 1555 proclamation confining them to either the Rome ghetto or to a second ghetto he established in the seaside port of Ancona. One can find remnants of their earlier presence in many small central Italian cities, such as in streets named *Via dei Giudei, Giudo* being the Italian word for Jew. They had been forced to abandon their homes and move to ghettos.

The memory of life before the ghetto also lives on in the surnames many Italian Jews were required to take; surnames such as Segni, Terracina, Tagliacozzo, Pontecorvo, Montefiore, Sinigallia, Ascoli D'Ancona, Viterbo, *etcetera*—all towns in the central Italy area that was once part of the Papal State. My great-grandmother Elisa Orvieto, born in Florence, was one such example. Orvieto is a lovely city halfway between Rome and Florence. It is interesting to think that her ancestors might have fled the Papal State, lived long enough in liberal Orvieto to acquire it as a surname, and then moved on to the still more liberal Florence.

However, Catholics employ many of these surnames as well, so one should not assume that those possessing them are necessarily Jewish. The only sure or quasi-sure common Italian Jewish surnames are Cohen and Levi, universally recognized as being almost exclusively Jewish.

As for my own ancestors, Italy has no town named Segrè, but France does, and Spain has an Ebro River tributary of that name but without the accent. Segres and Segrès might have a common origin. Some ancestors may have decided to distinguish themselves by adding an accent or, conversely, the Segres may have been Sephardic traveling East while the Segrès were Ashkenazim making their way South.

While my grandfather was a Segrè, my grandmother was a Treves, a surname with a certain Sephardic ring that is almost certainly misleading. My great-grandfather, Marco Treves, was born in Vercelli, one of those small Piedmontese towns that provided refuge to Ashkenazi Jews fleeing persecution in France or the Rhineland. A little sleuthing lends credence to Treves' Ashkenazi origins, as Germany's oldest city, Trier, was once named Treves, and before that it was known as Augusta Trevirorum, in honor of Emperor Augustus's conquest of the native *treviri* tribe.

Occasionally having a city surname led to amusing situations. Renzo and Lucia are the names of the hero and heroine of the acclaimed Italian novel, Manzoni's early-nineteenth-century masterwork *I Promessi Sposi* (*The Betrothed*). When my father's cousin Lucia Modena married Renzo Ravenna there were many knowing smiles. The appropriateness of a Renzo-Lucia real-life wedding grew when the newlyweds announced that they planned to live in Ferrara, Renzo's hometown, which lies roughly halfway between Modena and Ravenna. Smiles broadened at the thought of Lucia Modena and Renzo Ravenna positioned between their namesakes. It was obviously a meant-to-be match.

My father became less amused by this match when he discovered that his cousin was marrying an ardent Fascist. Perhaps it should not have been surprising. Renzo's hometown of Ferrara was an agricultural center and many of its Jews had become large landowners. Renzo was a lawyer and the landowners were his clients They were almost all wary of Socialist-leaning workers; Fascists promised they knew how to keep the status quo.

In 1926, thanks to a close friendship with a rising star in the Fascist Party, Renzo was chosen as Ferrara's *podestà,* the Fascist equivalent of mayor. It was a five-year appointment conferred by Roman bureaucracy rather than a local election. Renzo was the first Jew to be so chosen. He was honest, an able administrator, and loved his native city. In turn, the city was apparently content to see him reappointed five years later, and then once again five years after that. By then times were changing, and Renzo's being Jewish was making him unwelcome in the increasingly anti-Semitic Fascist hierarchy. He resigned a few months before 1938's passing of the Racial Laws that would have led to his immediate dismissal.

Renzo's son Paolo was far more critical of the Fascist era than his father. In time he became a Ferrara lawyer, a great contributor to the region's cultural life and to the uncovering of its history, with particular emphasis on its Jewish past. He shared many of those activities with an old friend, who had moved to Rome but kept returning to his hometown of Ferrara. He and that friend were instrumental in their city becoming the home of the National Museum of Italian Judaism and the Shoah.

That friend, Giorgio Bassani, was twenty-two years old when the 1938 Racial Laws forced him out of university. He soon took the only job he could find, that of teaching literature in the special Jewish schools established in Ferrara. There, he and his bright young student, Paolo Ravenna, formed a special bond. It continued through the years, as Bassani went on to become a famous author. His best-known work is a collection of five fictional stories of varying length about Jewish Ferrara, one of which has a thinly veiled critical portrayal of Renzo. The most famous of the five stories, "The Garden of the Finzi-Contini," became an international best-seller and was made into an iconic Italian movie.

CHAPTER 5

The Winds of Tolerance and Freedom

REVOLUTION and turmoil were sweeping through much of Europe and America toward the end of the eighteenth century. Talk of freedom was in the air and Jews were beginning to feel their time might be coming. The first official action that spelled out new liberties for them was Holy Roman Emperor Joseph II's 1782 Edict of Tolerance. However, the edict's primary goal, as clearly stated in its prologue, was to make "...the Jewish population useful to the state." Jews did have new rights but they were also expected to conform to new rules, such as no longer being allowed to speak Yiddish or Hebrew in public.

The Edict of Tolerance continued to exert its influence long after the Holy Roman Empire's demise, since a substantial portion of the empire survived in the form of a newly constituted Austro-Hungarian Empire (often simply known as Austria). The edict remained in effect throughout the new empire's territories, which included much of Northern Italy (and, accordingly, all Jews living there). The edict was also adopted in Tuscany because the ruling Archduke there belonged to a branch of the Habsburg family, and his cousin, Emperor Joseph himself, had passed the edict. He felt he had no choice.

The French Revolution of 1789 caused a more radical transformation in the relation of the Jews to the state. In August of that year, France's rapidly formed National Assembly issued a Declaration of the Rights of Man that was broader than the Edict of Tolerance, though, like the edict, it had features that Jews greeted with ambivalence. New professions were indeed open to them, but others—principally moneylending—were now severely limited.

Napoleon's numerous incursions into Italy were also significant to Italian Jews, starting in 1796 when the Little General led a French army into Italy. He was greeted with considerable enthusiasm by the Jews whom he freed from ghetto life. This response was often tempered, however, by the backlash of Christian Italians' resentment of French occupation.

More than ten years later, now as emperor, Napoleon marched on Rome and took control of the Papal State, doing away *inter alia* with Rome's ghetto and giving Jews full rights. The pope, Pius VII, excommunicated him, but, imprisoned by Napoleon, he was without any power. For a brief interlude the Jews of Rome lived well. However, that changed in 1814 when an alliance of nations defeated Napoleon and he was exiled to the island of Elba. Italy returned to its prior societal structures, including the pope as head of the Papal State. Ghettos were reinstated and the city's Jews were again confined. Napoleon's demolition of ghetto walls had been an important but short-lived event in the history of Italian Jews.

Thirty years later, the hopes of Roman Jews rose again when the reportedly tolerant and forward-looking Giovanni Ferretti was chosen as pope. He soon proved such optimism warranted. In 1848 the holiday of Passover began on the 17th of April. On that very night, without previous notice, the pope had the ghetto's walls demolished. Soon afterwards, rejoicing in their new freedom, Rome's Jews began to open stores outside of the ghetto and to integrate their lives into that of the city.

But citizen uprisings in November of 1848 showed that Ferretti, now known as Pius IX, was not liberal enough for the Roman population at large. Intent on joining the populist movements sweeping through Europe that year, they revolted against papal rule and installed a republican government in its place. Fearing for his safety, the pope fled Rome. Having previously made an alliance with France, he called for its troops to restore him to power. They quickly quelled the uprising, ensuring that the Roman Republic was short-lived.

The Pius IX that returned to Rome was not the Pius IX of old. The times were turbulent, and the Papacy reflected that. The ghetto walls were rebuilt and Pius IX began issuing a string of conservative decrees, culminating in 1864's encyclical *Quanta Cura.** Its appendix was particularly disheartening to those hoping for changes in the Church's perspective on the contemporary world and more specifically on the Jews. Called "The Syllabus of Errors," it consisted of eighty propositions, each attacking a trend of modern times. Secular education, civil marriage, and religious tolerance were all condemned. The Syllabus's final proposition asserted it was a mistake to believe that "The Supreme Pontiff can and ought to reconcile himself and come to terms with progress, liberalism, and modern civilization."

The pope had been making life hard for those Catholics intent on having the Church embrace more progressive positions for a long time. Some Roman punsters began referring to him as *Pio no-no,* a play on words for *Pio nono,* Italian for Pius the Ninth. The 1858 case of an abducted six-year-old Jewish boy, Edgardo Mortara, was an example of the church's rigidity. A young servant girl working for the Mortara family in their Bologna home secretly baptized Edgardo while he was sick in bed with a fever. She had done so out of fear he might die; in such cases the Church permits a layperson to give a very simple baptism. When she reported what she had done to her confessor, he passed the information on to higher-ups in the Church, who in turn consulted Rome.

Since the Church forbade raising a Catholic child in a Jewish family, the order that came back was that Edgardo must be

*A papal encyclical is a communication from the pope that is meant to clarify important issues for Catholics and guide them in their behavior. It is generally more discursive than the more formal declarative papal bull.

taken from his family, brought to Rome, and raised as a Catholic. As the event occurred in a city then still part of the Papal State, the order was carried out by the local police. Such actions had not been uncommon in the past, but Edgardo's abduction led to general outcry. It became an international scandal. Pius IX's response was that Church doctrine allowed him no alternative.

The pope's adherence to strict and seemingly antiquated interpretations of Church scriptures was again on display in 1869. There was much anticipation for his summoning of the world's cardinals and bishops to Rome for an ecumenical council. Some thought Pius might want to double down on his positions, while others expected he would propose leeway in the interpretation of the Syllabus of Errors—a hope that was quickly dismissed. He asked the clerics to approve a decree stating that the pope was infallible when speaking on matters of faith or morals. After the measure was accepted—reluctantly, by many—Pius IX called a for a few months' respite in the council's meetings.

By the mid-1860s, Italy was an almost unified country and the new Kingdom of Italy had already been proclaimed. Many Romans were now thinking they would be better off as part of the new kingdom rather than being ruled by a pope. The city's Jews certainly felt this way. Jews were gaining full rights everywhere else. When would Rome's time come?

CHAPTER 6

The Beginnings of the Golden Age

THE moment they were waiting for didn't come in Rome until 1870, but by then the new golden age was well underway for the country's other Jews. It was manifested by the end of ghettos and newfound assimilation and acceptance into Italian society and its economic and political realms. This golden age had gone hand in hand, since 1848, with the concerted social and political drive for Italian unification known as the *Risorgimento*. The movement had not truly gathered steam until the 1848 uprisings supporting it swept through Italy, but afterwards it grew rapidly, particularly in a region of northwest Italy nestled under the Alps, named *Piemonte* or Piedmont. In 1861, Turin, the capital of Piedmont, became the first capital of the new Kingdom of Italy.

The kingdom's roots lay in the early fifteenth century, when local nobility had merged their small holdings together. The union they formed was named the Duchy of Savoy, then renamed the Kingdom of Sardinia after its eighteenth-century acquisition of the island of Sardinia. However, even after the Duke of Savoy became the King of Sardinia, his region's capital remained in Turin.

As the Duchy of Savoy was formed, a comparatively large Jewish population began settling there, almost all Ashkenazim seeking refuge after expulsions from France and from the Rhineland. By 1600, Ashkenazim Jews lived in forty or so small towns scattered throughout the region. The Sephardic migration from southern Italy and Spain did not reach Piedmont until later.

The synagogues that remain from around 1600 are often located on an upper floor of an unmarked house to avoid vandalism. Unassuming from the outside, the synagogues' interiors were frequently lavishly decorated, a mark of the wealth the Jewish communities were managing to accumulate. Many of these synagogues were abandoned in the late nineteenth century when Jews moved from the small towns to larger cities such as Turin or Milan, but the ones surviving give an idea of their original splendor and of their importance to the communities that once worshipped in them.*

Despite many restrictions, Jewish life in these communities remained freer than elsewhere in Italy because Piedmont, nearly as far away from the Papal State as one could be in Italy, initially resisted pressure from the pope to move Jews into ghettos. Eventually it gave in and ghettos were formed. But the currents of freedom initiated by Holy Roman Emperor Joseph II and then by the French Revolution at the end of the eighteenth century took firm hold.

Carlo Alberto, King of Sardinia, was aware that the pope had been chased from Rome in 1848. He also saw his nearby neighbor, King Louis Philippe of France, forced to abdicate and then sent into exile. Lest he suffer a similar fate, Carlo Alberto issued a constitution for his kingdom, the *Statuto Albertino* (Albertine Statute).

The statute, now recognized as the foundation of constitutional monarchy in Italy, stated explicitly that all the kingdom's citizens were equal before the law, all had access to civil and political office, and all were eligible for military service. It also granted freedom of the press and personal liberty through the right of *habeas corpus*. This document had lasting import. In 1861 it became the Kingdom of Italy's constitution and remained as

* The synagogue in Casale Monferrato, a Piedmontese city of little more than thirty thousand inhabitants, has been restored to its former glory and is now a national monument. Built in 1595, it is considered a jewel among that era's places of worship.

such, essentially unchanged, until the Fascist era. Significantly, although the statute proclaimed Catholicism as the Kingdom of Sardinia's official religion, it also guaranteed freedom of worship. In retrospect, the passage of the *Statuto Albertino* is the major marker for the arrival of a golden age for Italian Jews.

Unfortunately for Carlo Alberto, his ambition to add adjoining Lombardy to his kingdom led him to declare war on Lombardy's ruler, the mighty Austrian Empire. Suffering a resounding defeat, he was forced to abdicate in favor of his son and go into exile. But this son, who took the name Victor Emanuel II,* was successful where Carlo Alberto had failed. After little more than a decade he was crowned King of Italy, and reigned over an Italy that looked much more like the present one than the hodgepodge of countries it had been in 1848.

The *Risorgimento's* triumph and the accompanying Jewish progress owe more to three extraordinary individuals than to King Victor Emanuel, who all too often showed more interest in women and game-hunting than in politics. The three are Giuseppe Mazzini; Camillo Benso, Count of Cavour; and Giuseppe Garibaldi. Born in Genoa in 1805, Mazzini was five years older than Cavour and two years older than Garibaldi. The trio are sometimes known as the heart, the brain, and the sword of the *Risorgimento.*

A steadfast believer in republicanism and a prolific author, Mazzini was unwavering in his condemnation of materialism and preached the need for freedom from tyrants. His central tenet, expounded clearly in his 1860 *I Doveri dell'Uomo* (*The Duties of Man*), was that life should be dedicated to others, to making them and oneself into better people, not to the pursuit of power or personal happiness. These beliefs led him to

* When sworn in as first king of the *Regno d' Italia* in 1861, Victor Emanuel insisted on being known as Victor Emanuel II rather than Victor Emanuel I. The former was the title he had previously held as king of the *Regno di Sardegna,* and he wanted to maintain it even after becoming Italy's first king. The decision was regarded as controversial.

participate in one uprising after another, to being imprisoned, and more than once to seeing his co-conspirators executed.

Cavour, the Kingdom of Sardinia's prime minister during the 1850s, was the ablest statesman Italy has ever known. He was responsible for the maneuverings that brought most of the northern half of Italy together into the single unit that in 1861 became the Kingdom of Italy. Cavour was its first prime minister.

The incorporation of southern Italy into the nascent kingdom arose through a seemingly quixotic mission led by Garibaldi. In the spring of 1860 this swashbuckling revolutionary, already famous for his military exploits in freeing regions of Italy and South America, began calling for volunteers to join him in a mission to overthrow southern Italy's ruling government, the *Regno delle due Sicilie.* In early May, with his troops loaded into two boats, Garibaldi set out from Genoa on what had come to be known as the *Spedizione dei Mille.* They landed in western Sicily a few days later, and, though initially only numbering a thousand or so, they were soon joined by reinforcements from all over Italy and even some foreigners. By September they had taken not only Sicily but all southern Italy, including Naples, and turned its control over to the new Italy.

Italian Jews, eager to participate in the *Risorgimento* struggles, managed to make significant contributions, well beyond their meager percentage of Italy's population. Several were among Garibaldi's *Mille.* Isaaco Artom was Cavour's personal assistant and later a diplomat, the first of many Italian Jews to play roles in national politics. Mazzini, who for many years was an exile in London, was often financed by Jews, assisted by them in making his ideas known, and eventually, still persecuted, he died in the home of a Jewish friend.

There is no Italian city of any size without a Via Mazzini, a Via Cavour, and a Via Garibaldi except for those who have chosen to honor one or more of the three by giving his name to a Piazza rather than a Via. On the other hand, the Italian monarchy's behavior, discredited by its behavior under Fascism, has made it impossible to honor Victor Emanuel II even if a city were inclined to do so. In the wake of World War II, cities that had used his name in the nineteenth century typically changed the Piazzas named after him to *Piazza della Libertà* or *Piazza dell' Indepenndenza.*

By 1870 Italy was almost completely unified except for the Papal State, and it, once extending past Bologna in the north and almost to Naples in the south, had been whittled down to a much smaller region centered on the city of Rome. That remnant was still protected by the pope's allegiance with France.

The 1870 Franco-Prussian war once again changed the balance of power. French troops urgently needed on that front were withdrawn from Rome, but France was defeated anyway. In early September, the country's emperor, Napoleon III, was deposed, and amidst general chaos, a republic was proclaimed in France.

Napoleon III had extracted a promise from Victor Emanuel II that Italy would not attempt to take Rome, but the Italian king now said he had made that promise to the emperor, not to the man. Since Napoleon III wasn't emperor anymore, Victor Emanuel II maintained the promise no longer held. The stage was now set for a head-to-head battle between the new Kingdom of Italy and the pope. The road to Rome was clear. By the evening of September 19, Italy's troops, amassed outside the city's wall, were completing their plans for ending the thousand-year-old papal control of the city.

After centuries of chaos and more than three hundred years of quasi-slavery, Rome's Jews knew that freedom and integration into Italian life would finally come to them, as it had to other parts of Italy. The stranglehold of the Papacy was being challenged and victory was in sight.

CHAPTER 7

The Final Battle for the Papal State

CAPTAIN Giacomo Segre, a thirty-one-year-old Piedmontese Jew, played a historic role in the battle for Rome.* He was a member of the first generation of Piedmontese Jews to grow up benefiting from the full rights granted in 1848 by the *Statuto Albertino.* He had graduated with an engineering degree from Turin's University and then enrolled in the army, both activities that would have been closed to him before 1848. Segre was proud of his achievements and looked forward to the day when his own children would become even more successful.

As dawn broke on the 20th of September 1870, the Kingdom of Italy's troops were making their final preparations for an assault. Their first task was to create a large enough opening in the city walls for soldiers to charge through. A little after five in the morning, General Cadorna gave the order to fire cannons at the city gate known as Porta Pia.

The fifth artillery division, placed only four hundred yards away from the Porta, controlled the bank of cannons nearest the target. Its commander, known as one of the finest artillery officers in the Italian Army, was none other than Giacomo Segre. In response to the order, he began firing immediately. The pope had warned that the first man who dared breach the walls of his city would be excommunicated. That did not worry Captain Segre. He was a Jew. The fortuitous circumstance of

*Despite the similarity in surnames and the smallness of Italy's Jewish community, he is not known to be related to my family.

Segre's religion and his considerable skill combined for a successful assault.

The early morning fighting was fierce, with Segre and his command coming under fire from snipers planted outside the city walls who could effectively target them. Segre lost two of his corporals and his trusted lieutenant. He wrote to his fiancée, Annetta, the next day, telling her about the battle and assuring her that he was unhurt.

It took almost three hours of bombardment to create an opening sufficiently large for the army's elite *bersaglieri* military unit to storm the walls with support troops by their side. The skirmish that followed the breach was relatively brief because the papal troops, most of whom were foreign volunteers, were outnumbered by a four to one ratio. The pope had thankfully said that bloodshed and destruction within the city should be avoided as much as possible. Therefore resistance, once the wall had been breached, was minimal. At 5:30 in the afternoon the head of the papal troops, General Kanzler, formally surrendered to General Cadorna.

Riccardo Mortara, a Jewish lieutenant in the invading Italian Army, created a special mission for himself that day. He hadn't seen his younger brother Edgardo for twelve years, ever since the Bologna police had taken him, then only six years old, away from his family to be raised as a Catholic in Rome. Riccardo raced through the city to find his brother. The meeting did not go well. In the intervening years, Edgardo had become devout, eventually entering the priesthood. The chasm between Jew and Catholic was too great to cross. Edgardo shunned him as an enemy. Riccardo's reception at the ghetto was quite another matter. Its residents were overjoyed to meet a Jewish lieutenant in the army that was liberating them.

At the end of the battle, Pius IX retreated to the sanctuary of the Vatican City. He called on Italy's Catholics to reject the usurper's illegitimate government, whose existence he refused to recognize. He then sent out an appeal to the world's

Catholics to restore him to power. Both pleas went unheeded. He also canceled all further meetings of the ecumenical council he had convened in 1869. Pius IX's religious power remained intact but his political power had collapsed.

In the following weeks Rome witnessed the beginning of another drama, though it might be more accurate to describe it as a farce. It revolved around finding a residence for King Victor Emmanuel II in Rome. The Quirinal, the pope's vacated city palace, was the obvious choice but Pius IX claimed it was still his property. He refused to turn over the keys to the building and went so far as to garrison a small detail of his troops inside to defend it against Italian intruders.

General La Marmora, a former head of the Italian Army, attempted to negotiate the Quirinal's transfer with the pope's Secretary of State, but it was to no avail; he was simply ignored. With a mini battle in the making, La Marmora arrived at the Quirinal's front door on November 9 with troops and locksmiths. Opening the front gate, they proceeded room by room, finding one bolted door after another. In the end, the pope's troops left out the back door. There was no confrontation, the rooms were empty, and the only real work done that day was by locksmiths.

The next set of problems the new Italian Government faced was when Victor Emanuel should arrive in his new capital and who would officially welcome him. Bad weather put an end to the dilemma. On the 28th of December, 1870, Rome suffered the greatest rainfall and flooding in two hundred years. The clergy maintained that God was expressing his displeasure with the year's events, but the king's entourage thought it was a blessing. It provided a way to make his first visit to the city short and unobtrusive.

He arrived in Rome by a special train, early on the 31st. Once inside the Quirinal, the king greeted a small crowd gathered in front, making sure to address them from a window other than the one the pope had habitually used. He promised the citizens of Rome standing outside that a fund would be made available to counter the disasters the flood had caused. He then had a good meal, took a little rest, decided on suggested renovations for the Quirinal and got back on his train. His whole stay in Rome had lasted thirteen hours.

And so 1870 came to an end and a new year began. The Jewish New Year 5631 had begun on September 25th, only five days after the battle that determined the end of Europe's last ghetto. Rome's Jews were now free to go anywhere, while the pope—admittedly of his own free will—had chosen to become a prisoner within the Vatican's walls.

CHAPTER 8

Two Deaths: The King and the Pope

PIUS IX continued to deny the Kingdom of Italy's legitimacy. In the years that followed his retreat into the Vatican, he occasionally even threatened to move the papacy to more friendly soil, perhaps France, Belgium, or Germany.

Attempting to win over the pope, the Kingdom of Italy's Parliament offered him many privileges, as well as a large annual income in perpetuity to the papacy. But the agreement stipulated that, in return, ownership of Church property would pass to the state, which would then also pay clerical salaries. Since acceptance would have meant recognizing the Kingdom of Italy's legitimacy, the Vatican rejected the offer.

Rome's old families, the Colonnas, Orsinis, Barberinis, Borgheses, and their like certainly did not want the papacy to move, nor did they welcome the king's arrival in their city. For centuries, their families had filled high offices within the Papal State governance and the clergy, and together they claimed at least a cardinal or two in their past and at times even a pope. Ennobled by one pope or another, they formed the *Nobiltà Nera* (Black Nobility), so named because its members always dressed in formal black.

They regarded the king, with his pretentious mustache and his many mistresses, as coarse and vulgar. They also did not want to mix with the *Nobiltà Bianca* (White Nobility), the group ennobled by the King of Sardinia or later by the King of Italy. That supposedly elite group even included some Jews. In the *Nobiltà Nera*'s eyes this was both an insult and a further confir-

Pope Pius IX by Adolphe Braun, 1875.
PUBLIC DOMAIN, VIA WIKIMEDIA COMMONS.

mation of the *Nobiltà Bianca*'s inferiority. An uneasy coexistence between the two groups set in.

Meanwhile, foreign diplomatic corps were arriving in Rome and infrastructure was being laid for the administration of what had become a large country, on par in size with France or Great Britain. Victor Emanuel II played the role he was expected to play as sovereign of such a nation until 1878 when he was struck by a high fever that quickly turned into pneumonia. He was fifty-seven years old at the time and had always been in robust health, so his sudden death early that year came as a shock to the new nation.

The king's impending death had led to a crisis. Catholicism says that a priest cannot administer last rites to someone who has been excommunicated, and the pope had excommunicated

Victor Emmanuel II, first King of United Italy, by André-Adolphe-Eugène Disdéri. public domain, via wikimedia Commons.

the king for his leadership in the assault on papal territory. But having the king die without receiving last rites would cause a major scandal that might harm both the Kingdom of Italy and the papacy. A solution to the problem needed to be found.

Furthermore, the king continued to be a devout Catholic, despite his excommunication, and believed he would to be condemned to eternal damnation if he did not receive the rites. Negotiations between Church and State began in great haste and an accord was reached that allowed the king's chaplain to deliver the desired forgiveness.

He died on January 9, 1878. Much preferring Turin to Rome, the king had asked to be buried in Turin's Superga Chapel, where dukes of Savoy traditionally had their tombs. His son Umberto, the new king, decided this would be inappropriate, since Rome was the nation's capital. He placed his father's tomb in a church adjacent to the city's Pantheon.

On February 7, 1878, less than a month after Victor Emanuel II's demise, Pius IX passed away. This was far less surprising, as he was almost thirty years older than Victor Emanuel. Pius IX's reign as pope had lasted a record thirty-two years. Elderly Roman Jews still remembered their optimism when he was first elevated to the papacy, since he seemed to represent liberalism and religious tolerance.

The death of these two pivotal figures in the struggle for Italian unification led to a gradual relaxation of the tension between the kingdom and the papacy, but the Vatican's formal recognition of its old enemy did not come about until Mussolini. His Fascist regime negotiated a *rapprochement* in 1929, one that tied the Catholic Church to the Italian State. While some citizens approved of this, others felt it was problematic. Little did they know how problematic it would become.

CHAPTER 9

Rome's Jewish Mayor

WHEN ROME became the nation's capital, Italy found itself with another problem on its hands in addition to the tension between the pope and the king: that of administering a city that for the first time in hundreds of years was growing rapidly. Room had to be found for the installation of a parliament, foreign embassies, offices for a massive new bureaucracy, and housing for all the personnel that went with these measures. The problem was magnified because Rome was full of priceless remnants of a great civilization, many of which were buried underground. Digging new building foundations required permits unlike those in any other growing metropolis.

A city council was formed, but the choice of a mayor for Rome was put in the hands of the political party that ruled the country at the time. This system was replaced in 1890 by one better designed to be in Rome's best interest: namely, the mayor would be chosen by the city council. This format held until the Fascist takeover of city affairs in 1926.

In 1907 the council picked a Jew, a selection that underlines how rapidly Jews were being accepted not only in Italy but even in Rome. Pius IX would certainly have both feared and condemned this choice of mayor, for the individual in question seemed to have almost all the features he thought characterized the Church's worst enemies. In his 1873 encyclical, *Etsi Multa Luctuosa,* Pius had identified them.

> Some of you may perchance wonder that the war against the Catholic Church extends so widely.

> Indeed, each of you knows well the nature, zeal, and intention of sects, whether called Masonic or some other name. When he compares them with the nature, purpose, and amplitude of the conflict waged nearly everywhere against the Church, he cannot doubt that the present calamity must be attributed to their deceits and machinations for the most part. For from these the synagogue of Satan is formed, which draws up its forces, advances its standards, and joins battle against the Church of Christ.

Jews are not mentioned in the document, but it is clear who Pius IX had in mind. Given his concern with the threats posed by Freemasons, Jews, and other members of the "Synagogue of Satan," one can imagine what his reaction would have been to seeing Rome select Ernesto Nathan as mayor. Nathan was a Jewish, London-born, German-fathered, Grand Master of the Grand Orient of Italy's Masonic Lodge. Serving for six years, longer than any mayor before or since, many also think he was the best mayor Rome has ever had.

Nathan's entry into Rome city politics came in 1898 when he was elected as a city counselor. The city was spreading, and he was put in charge of dealing with the ruins being uncovered by excavations. This was a prickly issue for the expanding city because protecting those ruins threatened builders' intentions. Nathan did well in the position and, seeing the need for further reforms in how the city grew, the city council members chose Nathan as mayor. Since many working-class Romans were tired of seeing their municipality dominated by conservative Catholics, Nathan being a Jew may have helped advance his candidacy. He almost certainly had the support of the former ghetto dwellers.

Regulating land speculation through the development of a zoning plan was Nathan's first move. His next was to try to take control of schools away from the clergy and put it into the hands of lay educators. He knew this would lead to a clash with the Vatican and its supporters, but he was eager to face that challenge. Nathan did so forcibly in a speech he delivered in front of city dignitaries on September 20th, 1910, the fortieth anniversary of Rome's liberation from papal rule. The day had been made a national holiday, so a considerable crowd gathered to hear Nathan. He proceeded to denounce the clergy for wanting to continue the reign of ignorance and not taking into account the teachings of the intellect as well as the moral and social aspirations of civilization. Nathan went on to say that while Rome was under papal rule, the city had continually erected new churches while ignoring the building of schools, and added that he was seeing to it that this unfortunate situation was now changing. The reaction from the Vatican was immediate, with one Catholic newspaper saying that Nathan needed to be sent back to the ghetto.

ERNESTO NATHAN IN SAN FRANCISCO, 1915.
UNKNOWN PHOTOGRAPHER. PUBLIC DOMAIN, VIA WIKIMEDIA COMMONS.

Nathan, a small, dapper, somewhat foreign looking gentleman, was not imposingly dignified like many Italian politicians of the time, but he was organized, efficient, and determined. A zoning plan that put an end to uncontrolled construction was approved, schools were improved, and funds from a significant increase of taxes on the wealthy were directed to the needs that he perceived as being paramount to the city: childcare centers, kindergartens, healthcare clinics, electrification of housing, a trolley car network, and public markets.

Common citizens developed a special affection for Nathan, reflected in a Roman dialect saying they used when describing his mayoralty: *nun c' è trippa pe' gatti* (there is no tripe for the cats), tripe being the common low-cost food that was fed to cats. Apparently, when presented with his first city budget, he crossed out an item that said "food for cats" after being informed that the food was intended for the felines that chased mice menacing the city archives. He is reported to have then said that eliminating the food would make the cats hungrier and force them to do a better job of catching their prey, adding that if no mice were left, so much the better because this would mean the city no longer needed the cats.

Many Romans loved Nathan but, not surprisingly, some of the city's powerful leaders did not. In 1914 Prince Prospero Colonna di Palliano, who was more to their liking, was chosen to replace him as mayor. The following year, as World War I approached, Nathan volunteered for the Italian Army despite being almost seventy.

CHAPTER 10

The Mayor's Mother

ERNESTO NATHAN had arrived in Italy in 1860 from London with his family. He was fifteen, barely spoke any Italian, and his father had died only a year before. How did he become an Italian political activist? Both his remarkable Italian mother and the city of Livorno, a place central to the history of Italian Jews, are key to understanding how it happened.

During the Renaissance, while Florence, Siena, and Pisa flourished as great centers of art and culture, Livorno remained little more than a hamlet south of Pisa, its total population less than a thousand individuals. Connected to Pisa by a canal which emptied into the Arno River and flowed to Florence, Livorno served as a well-protected port on the Tyrrhenian Sea.

The turning point in Livorno's development came at the end of the sixteenth century as a result of a crucial decision by Tuscany's ruling family, the Medicis. They had seen how the Gonzagas in Mantua and the d'Estes in Ferrara, powerful rulers of nearby states, had invited Jews from other parts of Italy, from Spain, and from Northern Europe to settle within their walls. These Jews had brought with them commerce and contacts, as well as skills in financial transactions. The Duchies prospered by this infusion, and so did the Jews, their populations soon swelling in Mantua and Ferrara to two thousand individuals or more. Having observed these successes, the Medici decided to replicate it in their own Duchy of Tuscany. After all, even the popes had taken note of such possibilities. The Papal State's city of Ancona on the Adriatic Sea had been made into a commerce center and Jews were invited to settle there. It had become a key link for transactions with the Near East, largely because of the connections Jewish merchants had cultivated in other Mediterranean centers.

The Medicis knew it would be a more difficult time to begin such a venture because the rise of Protestantism in Northern Europe had led the Catholic Church to launch a Counter Reformation with a much less tolerant attitude toward Jews. Nevertheless, having decided to risk papal displeasure, the Medicis began encouraging Jews to settle in Livorno, offering them favorable conditions and making the city into a free port, a site where imports can enter without tariffs and customs declarations are simplified. This transformed Livorno from a sleepy little town into one of the Mediterranean's prime commercial centers.

Between 1591 and 1593, Ferdinando I, Archduke of Tuscany, sent messages known as *Livornine* to merchants throughout Europe and the Middle East, more specifically to Spaniards, Portuguese, Greeks, Germans and Italians, Hebrews, Turks, Moors, Armenians, Persians, and others, inviting them to come live in Livorno. It was a general invitation, but the message was clearly intended for Jews who had escaped Spain in the previous century. The *Livornine* proclaimed that settling in Livorno would lead to Tuscan citizenship and allow travel anywhere in Tuscany without special identifying markings, such as yellow stars. The invitation also stated explicitly that new arrivals could erect their own places of worship and there would be no forced baptisms.

The response came very quickly, especially from Portuguese and Spanish Jews. Livorno grew rapidly. Its Jews traded throughout the Mediterranean and as far north as England. Italian soon supplanted the new arrivals' original languages: Portuguese, Spanish, or a mixture of the two with Hebrew. By 1800, the number of Jews living in Livorno—only a dozen or so, two hundred years earlier—was nominally five thousand, and probably appreciably larger. Jews made up at least ten percent of the city's total population. Livorno had a Jewish quarter but no ghetto, and its new synagogue, second in size only to Amsterdam's, replaced the very modest one that had been built in 1603. Rome was the only city in Italy with a Jewish population of comparable magnitude.

Some Livorno families made a great deal of money by following the same path as other wealthy eighteenth-century European Jewish families. The formula was simple: 1) start in banking or in commerce with close family members as partners; 2) marry cousins or members of other rich families to preserve the wealth; and 3) invest in land holdings when sufficient fortunes have been accumulated.

Ernesto Nathan's mother, Sarina, was raised in this bustling community. After her mother died in 1830, her father, seeking an environment of prosperous Jews, sent his eleven-year-old daughter Sarina to live there. He felt that Pesaro, the small town on the Adriatic where the family had lived, was no place for a young Jewish girl without a mother and decided it would be better for her to stay with her mother's relatives, the Rossellis, a family that had flourished during Livorno's growth. Among his many reasons for sending her to Livorno, he thought it would be far easier for her to find a Jewish husband there when the time came to look for one.

When Sarina turned sixteen, an older cousin named Emanuele Rosselli, a successful commercial trader with several European offices, introduced her to Meyer Moses Nathan, a German Jewish businessman from Frankfurt. He was staying in Livorno on an extended business trip. Nathan was twenty years older than Sarina, but such age differences were not unusual at the time, and when he proposed, Sarina accepted. Soon afterwards the newlyweds moved to London, where both Nathan and the Rossellis had growing business connections.

Sarina and Meyer Nathan quickly began having a family; twelve children followed in rapid succession, nine boys and three girls: David, Henry, Janet, Adolfo, Ernesto, Harriet (who later Italianized her name to Enrichetta), Giuseppe, Filippo, Alfredo, Walter, Ada, and Beniamino.

Sarina, a woman of great energy, with a strong continuing attachment to Italy, also befriended many other Italians living in London, including a group who had been exiled because of their views on Italian independence. In time she came to know their charismatic leader: Giuseppe Mazzini.

In 1837, fleeing a death sentence in Italy, Mazzini took refuge in London after finding himself *persona non grata* in both Switzerland and France. As the years passed, Sarina learned more about him and the causes he espoused. Becoming a convinced believer of Mazzini's teachings, she hired one of his London associates to tutor her children and began thinking how she might help Mazzini and his followers advance their causes. When Meyer Nathan died suddenly in 1859, Sarina found herself a wealthy forty-year-old widow with both the will and the means to further those causes. Her first step was to move back to Italy with her children and reestablish ties with her Livorno relatives. These ties would literally continue into the next generation, with two of Sarina's daughters, Janet and Harriet, marrying Rosselli brothers and two of her sons, Ernesto and Filippo, wedding Rosselli daughters.

Within a few years, having become increasingly important as both a strategist and a financier of Mazzini's political activities, Sarina relocated to the movement's home base of Milan. Accused of conspiracy against the state and feeling threatened, she subsequently moved across the border to Switzerland and purchased a villa on Lake Lugano, welcoming there her fellows-in-arms.

However, as the years passed and younger Italian revolutionaries turned increasingly to Marx's ideas of class warfare, Mazzini came to be regarded as less relevant. His final years were particularly bitter. In 1868, leaving London after a thirty-year off-and-on residence in Britain's capital, he followed Sarina to Lugano. It is commonly believed, though undocumented, that at some point she and Mazzini had become lovers. He made one last trip to Italy at the beginning of 1872, traveling under an assumed name to avoid arrest. Growing ill, he took shelter in the Pisa house of Sarina's daughter Janet and her husband Pellegrino Rosselli. Mazzini died there on the 10th of March, 1872.

After his death, Sarina left Switzerland and took up residence in Rome, where her son Ernesto and daughter Harriet had recently settled with their families. Energetic as usual, she threw herself into philanthropic and educational ventures that embodied Mazzini's principle of dedicating one's life to helping others. She added her own emphasis on aiding women in need.

Sarina died on the 19th of February 1882. Every year after that, on the date of her death, all her children gathered in Rome to honor her memory. Her obituary carried only a single reference to her being Jewish, describing her as originally an Israelite, which was a common nineteenth-century distinction often used to differentiate between Judaism as a religion and Judaism as a race. The article claimed that Sarina's only and unalterable faith was in social justice, a characteristic Mazzini phrase applicable to many nineteenth-century assimilated Italian Jews.

Following in his father's footsteps, young Ernesto pursued business-related activities but was neither very successful nor very happy with his work. He therefore eagerly accepted an 1871 offer from Mazzini to help direct a newspaper he was founding, *La Roma del Popolo* (Rome of the People). The paper did not survive Mazzini's death a year later.

Ernesto Nathan assisted with the preparation for publication of Mazzini's numerous writings, which eventually ran to almost twenty volumes. He first took on the task to assist his mother, by then the sole proprietor of Mazzini's papers; after her death he took full responsibility for the enterprise. In the meantime, he was becoming involved with Italy's Republican Party, founded decades earlier by Mazzini. It had recently split into factions;

one opposed any participation in the monarch-led Italian Government and another formed as an opposition wing within Parliament. In 1892, backed by this wing, Nathan ran for a seat representing Pesaro, his mother's birthplace. He lost narrowly, but by then he was also becoming active in Rome's city politics.

CHAPTER 11

Two Jewish Barons Study the Mafia

If Ernesto Nathan had won that seat in Parliament, he would have joined two other Jews, Sidney Sonnino and Leopoldo Franchetti, who had backgrounds resembling his own. The three were all the same age, had close Livorno connections, and came from wealthy families. Both were also sons of barons, their fathers having been ennobled by Victor Emanuel II because of their extensive philanthropic contributions. One of the two also had a foreign parent. Sidney Sonnino's mother was Welsh, so he, like Ernesto, was fluent in English.

There were, however, important ways in which these two were different from Ernesto. They had grown up in Florence, not London, had attended university in Pisa instead of going directly to work, and had both been members of Parliament for a long time before Ernesto's unsuccessful run for a seat. They were also staunch supporters of the monarchy, even though, like Ernesto, they were progressive on social issues.

In later life the two would be known as Baron Leopoldo and Baron Sidney; the titles bestowed on them after their fathers' deaths, even though they were not oldest sons. Italy had the custom of allowing all male children to claim the title of their forebearers.

During the 1820s, Sidney's Livorno-born father, Isacco Sonnino, had gone to Egypt's port on the Nile of Alexandria to seek his fortune. Quickly establishing himself in its finance world, he rose to considerable prominence in the service of Egypt's de facto governor, Muhammed Ali Pasha. Sonnino, close to forty years old, proposed marriage to nineteen-year-old Georgina

Menhennet, a Welsh merchant's daughter who also lived in Alexandria. She accepted and they had two children in quick succession. Since Muhammed Ali Pasha's four-decade term in power was nearing its end, and as they had already accumulated considerable wealth, the Sonninos decided to move to Italy, settling first in Pisa, where their son Sidney was born, and then in Florence.

Young Sidney showed early signs of exceptional brilliance at the University of Pisa, where he obtained his law degree at age eighteen. Throughout his career, many would accuse him of being too rigid, too intolerant, some even said too *Breetish*, but nobody ever doubted his intelligence or questioned his integrity. If anything, they argued he had too much of both for his own good, certainly for succeeding in his first career choice of diplomacy. Stationed in succeeding years in Madrid, Berlin, Vienna, and Paris embassies, Sonnino's linguistic ability and his keen mind were appreciated, but it became increasingly clear to him that diplomacy was not his calling.

Resigning from the service, Sonnino went back to Florence in 1871 and soon began to take an interest in land reform. He was prompted to do this because his father, like many wealthy Jews of that era, had invested in the purchase of large tracts of land. This brought Sonnino into contact with an old friend with similar interests, Leopoldo Franchetti, the grandson of Livorno merchants who had become rich from their business in North Africa.

In the early 1870s while Sonnino was studying Tuscan share-cropping practices, Franchetti was busy examining the farming practices in the Neapolitan provinces, part of Southern Italy that included the Abruzzi and Calabria. During trips he made in the region, he kept hearing the same complaints from locals. They lamented the combination of greed, malice, and ignorance in landowners, magnified by the fact that land in large estates was often owned by disinterested absentee owners. Farmers felt they had no political power and were hired only as day laborers. They also angrily maintained that it was all too easy for Northerners to say the land in the South was rich, and their Southern brethren were poor because they were lazy.

The two young men, deciding the situation needed to be documented, began planning an in-depth study of a single region in Southern Italy: they picked the island of Sicily. Accompanied by a friend and a single servant, they set out in early January of 1876. Traveling on horseback, they carried a minimum of supplies. Aware that they would often be staying in humble villages where banditry was common, their luggage included four rifles and four revolvers. They also carried folding cots, each one equipped with four small metal cups. When filled with water, these would act as traps and hopefully keep bugs from their beds.

Over the next five months they crisscrossed the island, interviewing people from all walks of life. Each night, they recorded memories from their encounters. The resulting two-volume book, *La Sicilia nel 1876* (Sicily in 1876), published just before Christmas that same year, has remained a classic. It included what was hailed as the best and most thorough study of the island's *mafia*. The book exposed the pervasive brigandage, feared and sometimes admired, that dominated most of the island and documented the reigning code of silence, *omertà,* in which one professes complete ignorance when questioned by authorities about alleged crimes.

The book's publication made Franchetti and Sonnino both well-known and appreciated in political circles, in part because an almost simultaneous government study of Sicily had produced a superficial analysis that completely whitewashed the region's problems. It was clear who had been thorough and who had not. Franchetti's and Sonnino's research could not be ignored because, far from being revolutionaries, they were progressive conservatives who fought for the rights of the agricultural poor. At the same time, they believed in Italy's monarchy and colonial holdings.

When the two young men returned to Florence, they started a weekly journal. Though it met with considerable success, within a few years the two decided to try effecting change from within rather than criticizing from the outside. In 1880 Sidney Sonnino won a seat in Italy's Chamber of Deputies, joining there his older brother, Giorgio. For six years, until Giorgio retired, the Chamber had two Sonninos as members.

SIDNEY SONNINO (1847-1922).
PUBLIC DOMAIN, VIA WIKIMEDIA COMMONS.

Sidney remained a deputy in Parliament for almost four decades, frequently holding additional important positions. He served twice as Minister of the Treasury, once as Minister of Finance, and twice as Prime Minister, a time in which he also held the post of Minister of the Interior. However, his most influential appointment was as Minister of Foreign Affairs, a post he held during the crucial five years of World War I and postwar negotiations.

Sonnino had a brilliant career, but he never achieved his dream of becoming the dominant political figure in early-twentieth-century Italy. That role fell to his Piedmontese contemporary, Giovanni Giolitti, a man whose influence was so pervasive that historians often refer to the Italian period between 1900 and the onset of World War I as the Giolitti Era. Many years later, reflecting in his *Memoirs,* Giolitti delivered an assessment of why Sonnino failed to achieve greater success.

> The honorable Sonnino, dedicating himself early in his life to politics and having entered Parliament while very young, and endowed with great will and extraordinary work capacity, prepared himself with a knowledge and understanding of the various branches of government administration that even those luckier than him never came close to obtaining. However, though he knew the problems, he never knew sufficiently the men whose collaboration, voluntary or forced, direct or indirect, is indispensable for the solutions to these problems in a democratic, representative government.

As Giolitti indicated, Sonnino was very skilled at devising solutions and in arguing his positions, but he was often unwilling to exercise the give and take of political maneuvering and failed to convince others to work with him. Each of his two terms as prime minister lasted barely three months, and his representation of Italy in post-WWI negotiations is widely considered disappointing, if not worse.

Part of Sonnino's inability, as Giolitti voiced, to *convince others,* was due to his character, but religion also played a role. He was regarded as an outsider. Even though Sidney's father had converted to the Anglican Church at his wife's request and Sidney was baptized at birth, many Italians still saw him as a Jew. Simultaneously, Jews did not recognize him as one of them.

Franchetti, whose background was conventionally Jewish, entered the Chamber of Deputies two years after Sonnino. His tenure in the Chamber, which lasted twenty years, was principally noted for his efforts to improve the lot of the agricultural poor, particularly in the Italian South. In the 1890s he led an effort to create favorable working conditions in the highlands of the East African colony of Eritrea, but that soon failed. Early in the twentieth century, he retired from the Chamber and increasingly turned his attention closer to home, to ameliorating the circumstances of the farmers on the large tract of land he owned in Umbria.

While Sonnino remained a lifelong bachelor, Franchetti eventually met a remarkable young woman, the slim, pretty Alice Hallgarten. Born in New York to wealthy Jewish parents, she moved to Frankfurt when she was ten years old to live with her uncle Charles after her father died. Franchetti met her when she moved to Rome to follow the Jewish tradition of charity, or *tzedakah,* and was working to improve living conditions for the impoverished. They married in 1900. She was twenty-six years old and, at fifty-three, he was more than twice her age.

Hallgarten's energy and devotion to aiding those in need energized Franchetti. Combining their primary social welfare interests, the newlyweds started a regional school for the children of poor farmers. A few years later, they visited the "Casa dei Bambini" located in Rome, where they observed Maria Montessori's innovative methods for teaching young children, aged three to six. Inspired by her approach, they invited her to conduct seminars for teacher training in their spectacular Umbrian villa, Villa Montesca, and helped her prepare and disseminate her educational philosophy. Her seminal book on the Montessori method, published in 1909, was financed by and dedicated to Baron and Baroness Franchetti.

Alice Hallgarten Franchetti died in 1911 when she was only thirty-seven. Six years later, Franchetti, who was prone to depression and still grieving the loss of his wife, committed suicide. World War I was then raging. The sudden catastrophic defeat Italian troops had suffered on the battlefield must have contributed to the despair that led him to take his life.

Franchetti left his estate to charity and his farm holdings to the men and women who cultivated his lands, with instructions that any debts toward him be forgiven in their entirety. Maria Montessori lived another forty years to become one of the most famous educational pedagogues of all time.

CHAPTER 12

Opportunity

IN 1909, while the Franchettis were bringing Maria Montessori's work to a greater public, Ernesto Nathan, then in his second year as Rome's mayor, was introducing many reforms to the city. His aim was to ameliorate the living and working conditions of the city's less privileged. Meanwhile, his friend Sonnino was about to have an even more dramatic influence on Italy's future. That same year, 1909, the king called on him to form a cabinet in the Chamber of Deputies and assume its leadership as prime minister.

1909 was less than fifty years after the proclamation of the Kingdom of Italy and less than forty after the kingdom's annexation of Rome. To understand how Jews advanced so quickly requires knowledge of what Italy was like in the aftermath of its unification, the opportunities Jews were offered, and how were they able to use them. Franchetti, Nathan, and Sonnino were only three of many Jews then rising to important positions in all aspects of Italy's political, social, and economic life. Each had the benefit of inheriting great wealth, but this was not so for all successful Jews of the era. An advantage for Jews at this time was that regional differences mattered less for them than for other Italians. Their common Judaism provided a shared link that transcended internal borders. A Roman might think of a Florentine as alien, but a Roman Jew would recognize a Florentine Jew as kin.

Italy in 1870 was still very much of a work in progress; its attempts to create a common identity remained fraught. It was not easy for the average Italian then to travel from one part of the country to another. Although the influence of Dante's *Divine Comedy* turned thirteenth-century Tuscan into quasi-official Italian, local dialect was often all an Italian knew how to speak. Furthermore, the common parlance varied so much from region to region that moving a few miles could be enough to make it hard to be easily understood. It was rumored that even the highly educated Cavour was more comfortable speaking French than Italian and needed help in writing the language of the country he led.

The lack of a common spoken language was one problem. Another was that while Italy welcomed the creation of their new kingdom, ancient regional loyalty caused friction. Piedmontese were far more like their French neighbors than like Sicilians. And distinctions could be even more fine-grained. Tuscans differentiated one city from another: Florentines identified as *Fiorentini,* as opposed to *Pisani* (from Pisa), *Aretini* (from Arezzo), or *Sienesi* (from Siena). These towns had fought bitter wars with one another centuries ago, and the memories of those battles were still fresh. There is even an Italian word for the promotion of one's own town, *campanilismo.* This is basically a claim that "my town's *campanile* or belltower is better than yours."

However, the country's outstanding problem was pervasive poverty. Lacking either iron or coal, and having little technical expertise, Italy remained a troubled agrarian country, one whose tracts of land were often in the hands of powerful nobility or of the Church. Almost seventy percent of the nation's work force made its livelihood in agriculture, but a farmer's life was one of pitiful subsistence. Eking out a living as a day laborer, a farmer and his family routinely owned nothing more than their simple hut. Tilling the soil improperly and without crop rotation had led to ever smaller yields. Modern farming tools had not yet been introduced, and there were now fewer arable tracts than in earlier times because extensive deforestation had caused topsoil to be washed away. Sicily was known in antiquity as the granary of Rome because of its wheat production, but this designation had long disappeared by 1870.

In the decades following the unification of Italy, the country's health suffered greatly. Malaria was the most pervasive problem. The disease manifested itself in a particularly virulent form along Italy's west-central coast, a region stretching from Tuscany to well south of Rome. It is estimated that in the last decades of the nineteenth century, there were two million cases of the disease annually, with an average yearly fatality of fifteen to twenty thousand individuals in Italy. In addition, the danger of malaria meant that some five million acres of farmland remained uncultivated, or cultivated inefficiently, because of the profusion of mosquitoes in those areas. Cholera was also a scourge. Italy witnessed six major epidemics of the disease during the nineteenth century, with a particularly severe one in 1867 killing more than a hundred thousand Italians.

The all-too-common occurrence of women dying in childbirth contributed to an imbalance between the number of women and men in the population. Infant mortality, the percentage of children born that did not live beyond their first birthday, was almost twenty-five percent. Malnutrition was common. The upshot of all these woes was that life expectancy in Italy was just under thirty years, ten or more years lower than in developed nations like France and Great Britain.

Not surprisingly, literacy was also less in Italy than in its northern neighbors. Only thirty percent of the population knew the basics of how to read and write, a figure somewhat higher in men than in women and higher in the North than in the South of Italy. The percentage of the population with some fluency in anything beyond the rudiments of arithmetic was even lower.

Most Italians were also denied the right to vote because the country's leaders felt an impoverished, largely illiterate population was not fit to determine the nation's course. The required qualifications for voting were being male, twenty-five or over, and having paid at least forty lire in taxes the previous year. Only two percent of the country's almost thirty million inhabitants met those criteria. In November of 1870, a scant two months after the breach of Porta Pia in Rome, a general election was held for Parliament's Chamber of Deputies, Italy's chief governing body. Only about half of those who were eligible to vote cast a ballot. Accordingly, the 508 Deputies were selected by only slightly more than two hundred and fifty thousand voters. In many cases a few dozen votes had been enough to swing a local election one way or another.

The Industrial Revolution had bypassed Italy. Rome, a city with a million inhabitants when Augustus was emperor, had shrunk to a population of 200,000. Paris' total had grown to two million by 1870. London, much smaller than Rome a few hundred years earlier, was now a metropolis of almost three and a half million inhabitants. It had also become the world's leading financial and commercial center, as well as the center of the British Empire. Even New York City had a size and dynamism no Italian city could dream of containing.

The difficulties the country was laboring under indicate the opportunities that were available for the country's Jews, compared to other Italians. Their rate of literacy was considerably higher than the national average, and Jews, with their early emphasis on learning, were more likely to have pursued education. Moreover, the only careers open to them in ghetto life—commerce and moneylending—encouraged skills such as bookkeeping and accounting, which were valued in a modernizing society. Ironically, their expulsion from Southern Italy hundreds of years ago and their subsequent settlement in Northern Italy worked in their favor, since the North of Italy was progressing faster than the South in every measure.

Post-unification Italy was a nation with many problems, but these problems created opportunities for improvement. Jews with full civil rights were eager to contribute. By the beginnings of the twentieth century, they had become mayors of major cities, generals in the Army, leading politicians, wealthy landowners, and successful academics. The emerging nation of Italy had provided an ideal climate for Jews to succeed.

CHAPTER 13

Acceptance

IN THE BEGINNING of the nineteenth century Italian Jews were beginning to see themselves welcomed. By the end of the century, acceptance was almost complete. The fact that Jews never made up appreciably more than one part in a thousand of the total population made it easier. Accepting them didn't cause major dislocations. Moreover, unlike in countries such as France, Germany, or the faraway United States, almost none of the Jews fleeing Eastern Europe's pogroms were arriving on Italy's shores. This meant that its Jewish population retained its long-time familiarity. Italian Jews looked like other Italians, dressed like them, and had fought by their side in the country's wars of independence. Having no separate language such as Yiddish, they also spoke like other Italians. Nor did the old canard of an "international conspiracy to control the world" take hold in Italy because, though its Jews were successful in many financial ventures, none acquired the intimidating reach of the Rothschilds or the Warburgs.

It may seem strange that Jews would be widely accepted in Italy, the world's Catholic country *par excellence.* But we must remember the bitterness large sections of the country felt for the pope because of his opposition to the country's unification and his insistence on keeping control of the Papal State. Most members of the political class felt this way but refrained from openly condemning the pope for fear of further exacerbating the political situation. However Garibaldi, the public's greatest hero, felt no such compunctions. There is still some controversy as to whether he did or did not refer to Pius IX as a "cubic

LA LIBRE PAROLE

ILLUSTRÉE

La France aux Français!

REDACTION | Directeur : EDOUARD DRUMONT | ADMINISTRATION

LEUR PATRIE.

Cover of Edouard Drumont's "La Libre Parole" (1893).
PUBLIC DOMAIN, VIA WIKIMEDIA COMMONS.

meter of manure," but there is no doubt that he said the man was intent on enslaving his subjects. The antipathy was mutual.

Anti-Semitic messages—reports of Jews drinking the blood of Christian babies and the like—did appear from time to time in regional Catholic journals and in the national *La Civiltà Cattolica,* a Jesuit periodical arriving on the newsstands twice a month. Founded in 1850, it was strongly supported by Pius IX and often used to express Vatican views, but neither it nor the regional Catholic journals had a large readership, nor were they influential outside of narrow circles.

Italy did not have a newspaper like France's extraordinary successful anti-Semitic daily, *La Libre parole* (*The Free Word*). The paper's editor Edouard Drumont went on to publish the strongly anti-Semitic book *La France Juive* (Jewish France) in

1886. It became France's number one best-seller, eventually published in more than a hundred editions.

Nothing in Italy approached France's Dreyfus Affair, the political scandal that divided the country in the wake of trumped-up charges of espionage made against a Jewish French Army officer. And no Italian political party put forward avowedly anti-Semitic candidates the way Austria's Christian Socialist Party did with Vienna's turn-of-the-century mayor, Karl Lüger.

The Church even unwittingly played a role in the acceptance of Jews, since the Vatican continued to deny that the Kingdom of Italy was the peninsula's legitimate government. This worked to Jews' advantage because Italy, unlike France, did not develop a strong right-wing Catholic Parliamentary Party that needed to be appeased if government was to function smoothly.

But credit should also go to the Italian people for their relative lack of anti-Semitism compared to Northern Europe. One example is that the upper ranks of military officers, often closed to Jews in those countries, were open to them in Italy. In 1888 Giuseppe Ottolenghi became the first Jewish general of a European army, and in 1902 he was appointed as the country's Minister of War.

Higher education provides an even more striking example of Jews' inclusion. Since most Italian universities were public institutions, they were open to all qualified applicants. There was never a question of quotas, still a sore point well into the middle of the twentieth century for Jews in other countries, including the United States. The same held true for faculty positions; by the beginning of the twentieth century almost ten percent of Italy's university professors were Jews—a remarkably high number, given that they represented only a tenth of one percent of the overall population.

There was comparably high representation among members of Parliament, too. There were three Jews in the first assembly of the new Kingdom of Italy's initial Chamber of Deputies in

1861, and ten years later there were eleven, already two percent of the overall number of seats.

It took more time for Jews to reach government ministerial positions. The first to be offered such a post was a Venetian, Isacco Pesaro Maurogonato. He entered Parliament in 1866, the year Venice was incorporated into Italy. Seven years later the king asked him to become Italy's finance minister, but he declined the offer. When pressed to accept, he wrote the king that he would of course obey an order from his monarch but felt that the stringent limitations about to be imposed by Parliament on the Church's finances made it politically unwise for a non-Catholic to be the one imposing them. The king reluctantly agreed with him.

But within a few years it had become completely acceptable for a Jew to occupy any cabinet position, even at the highest level. By the time of World War I, two men with Jewish fathers and one whose parents were both Jewish had served as prime minister. Once again, comparison to France, a country with a similar overall population but with considerably more Jews, is telling. It had a comparable number of government cabinet reshufflings during the period from 1870 until World War I, but none of its prime ministers were Jewish.

The presence of Jews in Italian Government institutions is evidence not only of their acceptance. It also shows how successfully they had assimilated.

CHAPTER 14

Assimilation

ONE FULL Jew served as prime minister of Italy before World War I. His name was Luigi Luzzatti. Born in 1841, he grew up during the early decades after the *Statuto Albertino,* the 1848 edict that granted Jews civil rights in the Kingdom of Sardinia. For many of the Italian Jews of his generation, including Luzzatti, integration into the general society was accompanied by abandoning much of the religious orthodoxy of their ancestors. Having done this, these Jews did not feel the need to develop a form of Jewish worship more in tune with modern sensibilities, such as the Reform Movement that arose in Germany during the nineteenth century and spread through Northern Europe.

Yet, with some exceptions, they usually retained their Jewish identity, doing so largely in private but significant ways. Their closest friends were likely to be Jews and intermarriage with partners of other faiths remained relatively rare.

But their Jewish identities only became public when they were called upon to protest anti-Semitism, whereas their loyalty to a newly unified Italy was loud and clear. This often led Italian Jews when questioned to describe themselves as *italiani ebrei* rather than *ebrei italiani,* meaning they were Italians who happened to also be Jewish, rather than the other way around.

Luzzatti's well-documented life provides an interesting case study of his era's Italian Jews. He was born in the Venice ghetto and was therefore an Austrian at birth, for the city on the laguna—an independent republic for many centuries—had come under Austria's control at the end of the nineteenth cen-

Luigi Luzzatti (1841-1927).

BAIN NEWS SERVICE, PUBLISHER. PUBLIC DOMAIN, VIA WIKIMEDIA COMMONS.

tury. His father owned two workshops, one for making woolen blankets and the other for processing rough hemp. The Luzzattis were a devout, observant family for whom life seemed to alternate between work and synagogue. Young Luigi first attended a Jewish school and then a regular *liceo*; during this time, he was tutored in Hebrew and the study of the Torah. But, as he narrates in his autobiographical *Memorie*, at sixteen he had a spiritual crisis in which, unbeknownst to his parents, he symbolically broke the rule of fasting on Yom Kipppur.

After his crisis, Luzzatti began to read the Gospels, slowly developing a pantheistic credo that led him to accept all religious practices. He regarded them as superfluous but did condemn intolerance. Though by training an economist and a lawyer, religion continued to be a major interest throughout his long life. Luzzatti's voluminous writings even include a biography of St. Francis of Assisi, and his last major book was entitled, *God in Freedom: Studies in the Relation Between Church and State.*

Though he had wide-ranging interests and was not himself an observant Jew, his best friend was a Jew, he was married in a synagogue, and he never wavered in his fight against anti-Semitism. Writing in his later years to an old friend, he tried to summarize his position on Judaism as, "I have the greatest respect for my religion, even after having lost the fervor for it I felt in my youth, but when my Jewish origins are reproached or when Jews are persecuted, I return to feeling and to declaring myself an Israelite....".

He served in Itay's Chamber of Deputies for fifty years, his tenure spanning the period from the 1870 liberation of Rome until the conclusion of World War I. During that half-century, he was the most prominent Jew in Italy's political life, several times Minister of the Treasury and once Prime Minister, but this was no sinecure. Italian Parliamentarians were not paid for their service until 1912, so life was hectic until then unless you were independently wealthy. While serving in the government, Luzzatti had to earn a living through his writings and by working as a law professor, first in Padova and later in Rome.

His commitment to a unified Italy later put him in direct conflict with the Zionist movement that was emerging in Europe toward the end of the nineteenth century. The main problem Zionism faced in Italy was its apparent conflict with identifying primarily as Italian. Luzzatti believed that humanitarian and philanthropic aid to other Jews was desirable, but any suggestion of mixed loyalties was not. As he put it, "I know only one homeland: it is where I was born, where my father was born, where I gathered my first impressions of the world and where I hope to die...There is only one. Jews are no longer a nation and Jerusalem is not their country."

CHAPTER 15

The Moncalvos

Luigi Luzzatti's best friend since childhood was a man named Enrico Castelnuovo. At the time of their birth, Venice had an overall population topping one hundred thousand and a thriving Jewish community of over two thousand—the only city in Italy besides Rome and Livorno to reach that number. When Austria took over Venice in 1798, the restriction that Jews must live in the ghetto was lifted, but two thirds of city's Jews stayed there anyway. Most of the others remained nearby because, with its five synagogues, the old ghetto was the community's center.

Enrico Castelnuovo's family circumstances were somewhat different from Luigi Luzzatti's, because his father had abandoned him and his mother when he was only eighteen months old, leaving them without a source of income, but it was still natural for two smart Jewish Venetian boys of the same age to become friends. However, poverty meant that Enrico had to leave school at fifteen and go to work as a clerk in a company belonging to his mother's uncle.

The bond between the two friends remained strong despite their diverging career paths, and it became even stronger in their twenties when Luzzatti married Amelia Levi and, soon afterwards, Castelnuovo married Emma Levi, Amelia's sister.

The young Castelnuovo family had two children in rapid succession, but Emma died after only four years of marriage. Enrico, who never remarried, raised the two children with the help of friends and relatives: his daughter Bice went on to be a successful painter and his son Guido became a prominent mathematician.

In addition to the personal tragedy of his wife's death, Enrico Castelnuovo's grand-uncle's business soon closed, but with Luzzatti's help he found a position as a teacher at Venice's business school, the *Scuola Superiore di Commercio.* Castelnuovo discovered that he enjoyed teaching and remained associated with the school until his death in 1915, never venturing very far from his native Venice.

Despite his family and teaching responsibilities, Castelnuovo found time to realize an early dream of being a writer. The next decades saw him bring forth poems, essays, short story collections, and a series of novels, all well received. Having them published by the Milan firm Treves Brothers was an added source of pride because their list of authors included not only Italian luminaries like Pirandello and Verga but, in translation, foreign writers he admired.

Castelnuovo's novels were read and appreciated because he had a good eye for the social foibles of his surroundings and a point of view that many appreciated.* All his writings show sympathy for the downtrodden and a certain nostalgia for the patriotic sentiments of the *Risorgimento,* the heroic era of Garibaldi and his comrades. The novels also condemned the new class of wealthy Italians that he found lacked a moral compass.

His last novel is of particular interest for the way it sheds light on turn-of-the-century Italian Jewish sensibilities and ambitions. Published in 1908 and entitled *I Moncalvo,* it deals

* Though widely read at the time, Castelnuovo is now not well-known. The only Italian novelist from his generation to have acquired an international reputation is Ettore Schmitz, a Jew whose father's family was German. Part of his education was in Germany, but he wrote in Italian, doing so under the pen name of Italo Svevo, an allusion to his mixed background, Svevo being the Italian word for Swabian.

with the lives of two brothers and their families; their surname of Moncalvo is that of the small Piedmontese town where their ancestors presumably once lived.

In the book's beginning, Giacomo, a widower and the oldest of the two brothers, has recently obtained a professorship of mathematics at the University of Rome. He is living with his son Giorgio, who has just returned from Berlin where he had been conducting post-graduate research in physiology, a first step in a promising academic career. Giorgio is pondering how life would have been different if he had heeded the advice his uncle, Gabriele, had given him when he was entering university. Assuring his nephew that he would become very rich if he followed this advice, Gabriele had told Giorgio to quit school, come work with him in his Cairo office, learn a little Arabic, and then go off to run his uncle's firm's Sudanese branch.

Many years pass, and Giorgio now meets his uncle again. Gabriele has amassed a huge fortune, decided to leave Egypt, and settled in Rome with his wife Rachele and their stunningly beautiful nineteen-year-old daughter, Marianina. On meeting her, Giorgio is thunderstruck, immediately falling in love. She is not indifferent to his attentions, but Marianina and her family have other ideas.

Gabriele and Rachele are social climbers. At one point he suggests to his wife that they could use their wealth to be ennobled, but she dismisses that possibility with a not-so-subtle reference to the likes of Sonnino and Franchetti, Jewish nobility. "There are too many of these financial barons. It is almost another mark of race." Rachele feels it would be a mistake to settle for this.

They hope that Marianina, thanks to her beauty and her very large dowry, will marry into the upper classes; this will give them their desired *entree* into society. But it may not be easy for, as Giacomo points out to his son, "she will have competition from her American girl friends. And they have more money than she does," a reference to the gossip that rich young women from the United States were coming to Italy in search of a husband with a title.

Gabriele and Rachele know they have the additional obstacle to moving up in society of being Jewish. Converting to Catholicism might be necessary and perhaps even desirable, but they think the first step should be to have Marianina make a good match. Having absorbed the Roman snobbery that ranks the old nobility as more prestigious than its Italian nouveau riche counterpart, they decide that nothing would be more advantageous than having her marry into the old strongly Catholic papal nobility, the *Nobiltà Nera.*

The plot now rapidly gathers speed. An elderly widow from such a family, Princess Olimpia Oroboni, lives across the street from the Moncalvos, together with her sickly, timid son, Don Cesarino. Having exhausted all their resources and being deeply in debt, their devoted elderly servants long unpaid, the Orobonis have fallen on hard times. The Princess has little hope of her son remedying this situation, for she believes he will never marry and will probably enter a monastery.

But, while out on his balcony at night, Don Cesarino catches sight of Marianina in her room across the street and is seized by a sudden passion, a veritable *coup de foudre.* Learning of this, a priest who is a confidante of the Orobonis and who Gabriele and Rachele have befriended, approaches the Princess. Having become aware of both Don Cesarino's sudden infatuation and knowing the Moncalvo's ambitions, he discreetly raises with her the possibility of a marriage between her son and Marianina as a solution to her financial problems.

She agrees to the match, though in an aside she says that if the likes of Marianina had tried to seduce an Oroboni four centuries ago, she would have been burnt at the stake. Marianina is excited by the prospect of marrying Cesarino. Her cousin Giorgio, who is in love with her, tries to dissuade her from going ahead with the plan, but Marianina rejects him, for she too wants the presumed triumph of marrying a prince of the *Nobiltà Nera.*

The wedding party gathers in the Papal Archbasilica of San Giovanni in Laterano. Marianina's baptism is scheduled to precede the marriage. During that ceremony the officiating priest intones, "What joy in Heaven for this victory of the faith! For this return to the Lord of the descendants of those that persecuted, derided, and crucified him." The wedding then takes place, after which the congregation hears the reading of a note from the pope. He is conferring his blessings on Marianina and Cesarino.

But as the carriage leaves San Giovanni, boys run alongside it yelling, "The Jewess, the Jewess," foreshadowing Gabriele's fear that despite the marriage, he and Rachele will always simply be regarded as Jews.

Marianina and Cesarino leave for a honeymoon in the Holy Land, and an anguished Giorgio falls sick but recovers and decides to go off to India to search for a cure for the plague afflicting the country, and Giacomo feels increasingly distant from his brother. Gabriele busily begins planning extensive renovations for the Oroboni *palazzo*—or rather, for all but the Princess's room. She has demanded it be left unchanged. There is a strong hint that Gabriele will destroy the *palazzo's* appearance and plunge its neighborhood into the profiteering that comes with urban speculation.

The book ends with Giacomo reading a newspaper report that details how Gabriele and Rachele, now generous donors to papal causes, will convert to Catholicism and simultaneously be honored by the Vatican.

Italian Jews reading *I Moncalvo* would recognize that Rachele is a caricature, but some of her assertions might have had a ring of truth for them, as when she states that, "Our grandparents were stubbornly orthodox, the next generation pretended to believe but they didn't, and we of the third generation couldn't have been raised in any other way."

The novel dramatizes the contrast between two goals that Italian Jews commonly pursued in late nineteenth century: making money and acquiring education. Castelnuovo makes his own preference between the two very clear.

CHAPTER 16

Castelnuovo's Son

AT THE BEGINNING of *I Moncalvo* we learn that Giacomo, Giorgio's father, has recently received a professorship at the University of Rome and has also been awarded the *Reale Accademia dei Lincei*'s prestigious gold medal—the *Lincei* being the Italian equivalent of Great Britain's Royal Society, though, if anything, more exclusive. Enrico Castelnuovo's choice for Giacomo's career was no accident. At the time of the novel's writing, Castelnuovo's own son Guido was both a professor in Rome and a recipient of the *Lincei*'s gold medal.

Guido Castelnuovo had become one of the stars among the many Jews who were then professors in Italy's universities. Their presence in academia, a hundred times greater than their percentage of the Italian population, provides probably the most conspicuous example of the advances of Italian Jews, as well as their assimilation and acceptance into turn-of-the-century Italy. By the time of World War I their contributions were significant in almost all academic disciplines, but mathematics was the only field they had come to dominate. It was also the sole branch of science in which Italy had achieved consistent world class status.

One reason Jews were so successful in mathematics was that they sought promising opportunities, and mathematics in the middle of the nineteenth century was just such a field. The country was becoming increasingly conscious of both the challenges and the possibilities mathematics offered, and strongholds of the discipline were emerging in the historic universities of Pisa, Turin, and, to a lesser extent, Padova, Pavia, and Bologna. But another factor may have also played a role in Jews gravitating towards this field. There wouldn't be favoritism or anti-Semitism in mathematics. You were either right or wrong.

No mathematician gained more fame in that Italian post-unification era than Vito Volterra. Born in Ancona's ghetto in 1860, his father died when he was two years old and he and his mother went to live with her brother, who was employed in Florence.

Vito's extraordinary mathematical ability was recognized at an early age and he shone at Pisa's elite *Scuola Normale.* His career was quickly launched, and he continued to surprise people with the breadth of his interests and achievements, attacking problems ranging from integral equations to population studies in biology. As his reputation rose, he also became extremely influential in all branches of Italian science. He was the founder and first president of the Italian Society for the Advancement of Science as well as the founder and first president of Italy's National Research Council, the organization charged with forging collaborations between science and industry. Volterra was not only a member but, after 1923, the President of the *Accademia dei Lincei.* Honors continued to be showered on him, both at home and abroad.

Turn-of-the-century Italian mathematics also had a great impact on physics, particularly through the work of another Italian Jew, Tulio Levi-Civita. His insights had been needed in the formulation of Einstein's General Theory of Relativity. Princeton University physicist John Wheeler, an expert on the theory, once jokingly observed that it could be summarized in a dozen words: "space-time tells matter how to move; matter tells space-time how to curve." Less succinctly, the theory examines the connection between viewing an object's path as due to gravitational forces or equivalently as the curving of the space and time in which the object is moving. Differential geometry,

Levi-Civita's field, provides the mathematical tools needed to describe the motion.

To formulate his theory, Einstein needed to learn techniques that Levi-Civita had developed with his Padova mentor Gregorio Ricci-Curbastro and then on his own. It hadn't been easy. As Einstein wrote Levi-Civita, who in the meantime had become a friend, "I admire the elegance of your method of computation; it must be nice to ride through these fields upon the horse of true mathematics while the like of us have to make our way laboriously on foot." In a more jocular mode, while he was condemning Italy's twentieth-century Fascist regime, Einstein once quipped, "There are two good things about Italy: spaghetti and Levi-Civita."

The 1919 observation of light rays from a distant star bending as they grazed the sun's surface during a solar eclipse agreed with Einstein's predictions. It made Einstein an international celebrity and drew further attention to Levi-Civita. That same year, he moved to Rome to take up a professorship at the city's *La Sapienza* university, joining Vito Volterra on its mathematics faculty.

The transfer was significant because it marked Rome's university's gradual transition from a backward educational institution to prominence as Italy's leading one. By the early 1920s, Rome had five internationally famous mathematicians on its faculty: all five were members of the *Accademia dei Lincei* and all five were winners of the *Accademia's* prestigious mathematics prize. Four were Jews: Volterra, Levi-Civita, Castelnuovo, and his dear friend Federigo Enriques. The fifth, Francesco Severi, was a Catholic.

Guido Castelnuovo, the novelist's son, graduated from Padova's University, the one Venetians usually attended. His field was algebraic geometry, the study of surfaces described mathematically by the zeroes of polynomials with several variables. That sounds esoteric, but it is central to much of modern mathematics. Establishing himself rapidly as a major mathematician, he obtained a position at the University of Rome in 1891 when he was only twenty-six years old. The following year he met Federigo Enriques, a twenty-one-year-old mathematician fresh from a degree at Pisa's *Scuola Normale.* Enriques, like many others in this story, was a Jew from an old Livorno merchant family. This meeting was the beginning of a historic collaboration in the history of Italian mathematics.

The two, with Castelnuovo a professor in Rome and Enriques one in Bologna, eventually became known world-wide as key to the founding of the so-called Italian School of Algebraic Geometry. Working in concert for more than thirty years, their correspondence extends to many hundreds of letters. Sometimes their results were reached during the long walks they took whenever they met. Enriques once quipped, perhaps referring to ideas generated in those walks, "Intuition is the aristocratic way of discovery, rigor the plebeian way." Decades later this style of thinking would be criticized, but their standing as giants in the field has remained.

When the Enriques family moved to Rome in 1922 for him to take up a professorship, they of course looked for an apartment near the Castelnuovos. There was more to it than just mathematical discussions, because in the intervening years Castelnuovo had married Enriques' older sister Elbina. The Enriques family found an apartment in the building where the Levi-Civitas lived. The Castelnuovo and Enriques families and their guests, including from time-to-time the Levi-Civitas and the Volterras, began gathering on Saturday evenings, the older members exchanging news in one living room while the younger ones gathered in a second living room to talk, play games, and, as they got older, sometimes even dance to gramophone records.

All seemed to be going well, but by the 1930s political differences were creating a split in the Rome mathematics department's faculty. The four Jewish professors, Castelnuovo,

Enriques, Levi-Civita, and Volterra were on one side and Severi on the other. The latter was energetic and talented, but combative, insecure, and jealous of rivals' success. Critical at first of Mussolini, he increasingly supported *Il Duce* and was rewarded for doing so. One example of this took place in 1929 when Mussolini created a Royal Academy of Italy, with large annual stipends for its members. He did this to supersede the *Accademia dei Lincei,* whose membership he could not control. He had veto power on the Royal Academy's appointments, and Severi was the only mathematician in its initial class.

The gap between the two camps widened in 1931 when, at Mussolini's insistence, the oath of loyalty to the king that all university professors were required to take was amended to include allegiance to the Fascist regime. The penalty for refusing was immediate dismissal. Severi was an enthusiastic supporter of the move, while Volterra was one of the twelve Italian university professors (out of a total of 1,250) who refused to take the oath. Five of the twelve were Jews, a fact surely brought to Mussolini's attention. Expelled from his university position, Volterra spent a good part of his remaining life abroad. He died in 1940. Castelnuovo, Enriques, and Levi-Civita hesitated, but in the end set aside their scruples and did take the oath. They, like many other professors, feared not taking it would lead to their being replaced by inferior mathematicians, chosen because they were Fascists, which would hurt students and damage the hard-earned reputation of mathematics research at Rome's university.

The divide in Rome's mathematics department continued to grow as the Severi camp increasingly took control. It became a chasm in 1938 when the new Racial Laws led to the Jewish professors being summarily dismissed from university teaching. Levi-Civita died in 1941, but Castelnuovo and Enriques tried to keep their teaching and research active in a special Jewish school. That came to an end in 1943 when they had to go into hiding. Other Jewish mathematicians, some already famous and some still only up-and-coming, had already scattered around the world or now followed their mentors' lead by hiding. A few of those who had departed returned to Italy after the war, but the Golden Age of Italian Mathematics was over.

Pro-Fascist mathematician Severi, who had asserted in 1938 that Rome mathematics would be fine without the likes of Castelnuovo, Enriques and Levi-Civita was suspended from his university position at the war's conclusion. Eventually he was reinstated but, shunned and embittered, he began making exaggerated and often unaccepted claims about his own research.

CHAPTER 17

The Lombardy Great Grandparents

MY GRANDFATHER Giuseppe Segrè, born in 1859, belonged to the same generation of Italian Jews as Volterra and, like him, identified as a Jew but was not an observant one.

Because of the complications of Italian politics during the year of his birth, he first saw the light as an Austrian but while still in his crib became French for an instant and then Italian. All these changes occurred because his birthplace was Bozzolo, a small town in southern Lombardy, about halfway between Mantua and Cremona. The region was the site of a short-lived 1859 war between Austria and France, who was allied with the Kingdom of Sardinia. Therefore, Giuseppe's parents were Austrian when he was born and briefly French at the war's conclusion because Austria lost but would only negotiate with France. It then ceded conquered Lombardy to the Kingdom of Sardinia, which would be renamed the Kingdom of Italy in 1861.

Jews had begun to settle in Bozzolo during the sixteenth century, probably seeking refuge from the Duchy of Milan, which, having come under Spanish rule, was then busy expelling its Jews. They were drawn to Bozzolo by its vicinity to Mantua, a city that was growing rich under the benevolent rule of the astute Gonzaga family. Like Venice, Mantua was welcoming Jews and also had multiple synagogues, each following different rites.

Bozzolo was one of the small towns clustered around Mantua that developed their own Jewish communities at that time, each containing only one to two hundred individuals but still big enough for them to support a synagogue and a Jewish cemetery. Records are scanty but do show that Segrès were operating small businesses there in the early 1600s. In any case, that is where my great-grandfather Angelo Miracolo Segrè was born, his unusual middle name of Miracolo (Miracle) owing to his mother supposedly being fifty at the time of his birth.

In 1845, twenty-six-year-old Angelo, who by then had his own shop in Bozzolo, married eighteen-year-old Egle Cases, the daughter of a relatively well-to-do Mantuan Jewish family. Over the next twenty years they had eight children; three sons and a daughter lived beyond infancy. Angelo and Egle looked no further than a good marriage for their daughter Bice's future but hoped for something more than life as a Bozzolo shopkeeper for their boys.

CHAPTER 18

Their Three Boys

Born in 1853, Claudio was the oldest of the three sons. His parents quickly recognized he was very smart and thought that a good education would be key to his getting ahead, but the only option for higher studies in Lombardy was Pavia's university. That made it a natural destination for Claudio, but almost all Pavia's students came from well-to-do families, and the Segrès, besides being Jewish, were anything but that.

Fortunately, Claudio learned of the *Collegio Ghislieri*, a small residential college attached to Pavia's university. Founded in 1567 by Pope Pius V, its mission was to provide promising boys from poor families with a good education before they entered the ranks of the clergy. Admission was competitive and acceptance meant room, board, and fees were all taken care of, as long as one did well. The requirement to become a clergyman would have ruled out Claudio's enrollment, but that restriction had ended with the eighteenth-century Austrian occupation of Lombardy. Probably the only Jew to apply for admission to the Ghislieri, he was accepted and graduated in 1874 with a degree in mathematics.

Claudio's next move was motivated by his increasing awareness that Italy's limited railroad system was a serious impediment to the country's modernization. In 1870, the country had only 6,000 kilometers of rail lines compared to France's 20,000, Great Britain's 26,000, and the United States' 96,000. The situation was already changing; ten years earlier, Italy's lines had been only 2,000 kilometers long and they were operated by two dozen different companies, some of which were foreign-owned.

By 1870 there were only five such companies in Italy, but they still lacked expertise on every front. Helping to fill this need would be a career that met Claudio's criteria: a great opportunity and the possibility to do something of real service to his developing country. But first he needed to develop expertise, so he moved to Turin to pursue a higher degree in engineering and geology and after that went to Paris for further studies at the elite *École de Mines*—all this on scholarships.

Returning to Italy, he joined the *Ferrovie Meridionali,* one of the five companies operating Italy's railroads. Founded in 1862 and headquartered in Ancona, a city with a rich Jewish history, it oversaw the lines on the Adriatic coast. Settling in Ancona, Claudio, a confirmed bachelor, was joined by his parents after his father closed the Bozzolo shop. Thanks to the city's Jewish community, they felt comfortable settled there. Though Claudio's father died soon after the move, his mother lived with him until her death in 1905.

In Ancona Claudio established and directed a special institute for the study of problems related to the production, maintenance, and operation of rail lines. He addressed how terrains and materials are chosen, routes are selected, rail lines are built, and how maintenance is implemented. His institute became both helpful and well known, but management problems and difficulties in coordinating the different lines continued to make railroad transportation unsatisfactory.

Matters finally came to a head in 1905 when Italy, following the lead of other European countries, consolidated its lines into a single nationalized entity, the *Ferrovie dello Stato.* During the next years, a complete turnaround of the financial status and a radical modernization of the Italian railroads' equipment took place. Riccardo Bianchi, an old friend of Claudio's from engineering school in Turin, was the person in charge.

In 1905 Claudio moved to Rome, taking with him the institute he had founded. It went on to develop an international reputation and, as its director, Claudio traveled throughout

Europe and the Middle East, helping others establish similar centers wherever he went. Even the academic community came to value him, and in 1926, two years before he died, he was elected to the *Accademia dei Lincei.*

My grandfather Giuseppe, the second son of Angelo and Egle, was more interested in business matters than attending university. He acquired some early commercial experience and then, still in his mid-twenties, he struck out on his own. Finding a way to exploit new-found electric power, then colloquially known as white coal, seemed to him the most promising avenue for getting ahead. His quest for a way to do so brought him to Tivoli, an ancient town about twenty miles east of Rome.

Known in antiquity as Tibur, Tivoli was already famous during the Roman Empire. Located at the point where the Roman countryside begins to turn into the Apennine hills of central Italy, and surrounded by magnificent groves of poplar trees, it is also graced by the cascading waterfalls of the Aniene river. The city is in a charmed location, cool enough in the summer to provide a respite from the heat of Rome and yet close enough to the capital to be easily reached in at most a few hours, even then. Attracted by its beauty, several ancient Romans built sumptuous villas in its vicinity.

But Tibur was more than a site for comfort and relaxation. Its greatest monument, predating its phase as a resort, was the Sanctuary of Hercules Victor, the war-like Roman god that Tibur adopted as its protector. Begun in the second century B.C.E., shortly after the Roman Republic had conquered the Greek peninsula, the sanctuary construction extended over forty thousand square feet. Its main feature was a rectangular expanse anchored into the hillside and supported there by massive buttresses that enabled it to stretch away from the hill. Over the centuries, most of the sanctuary disappeared—except for the buttresses. Even the surroundings became known as Villa di Mecenate, the Italianization of Maecenas, the noted Imperial Roman patron of the arts who had built a villa there.

Well into the Renaissance, the town now known as Tivoli continued to be a vacation retreat, marked by villas erected in the emerging style that emphasized sloping terraced gardens. Prominently featured were intricately linked fountains sporting waterworks, their jets emerging from the mouths of elaborately carved figures. Tivoli's Villa d'Este, dating back to the mid-sixteenth century, is regarded as Europe's finest example of such gardens. Now a UNESCO World Heritage Site, it makes full use of the hillside through a display of cascading water so striking it has made the name Tivoli synonymous throughout the world with pleasure garden, and in some cases it has even been adopted as the name of an amusement park.

Though the beauty of the surroundings may have stirred him, my grandfather was primarily drawn to Tivoli by the potential use of its waterfalls to generate hydroelectric power. In his mid-twenties he joined and soon became head of a company set up in 1886 to exploit this new source of power. Tivoli became the first city in Italy to be lit by electricity.

Another ambition moved my grandfather. He wanted to revitalize the modest local paper industry. He recognized that all the necessary ingredients were in place: forests that could yield the necessary wood pulp, abundant sources of water, electric power, and a nearby market for his products—the city of Rome. Making use of what was already in place, the paper mill was built on the ruins of an ancient villa. Though employing those rocks seems sacrilegious to our modern sensibilities, one must remember that much of Rome was built using antiquity's stones as a quarry. Nineteenth-century photographs show even the Forum's grounds being employed for growing vegetables and for animals' grazing. Nor is it uncommon to still notice pieces of ancient Rome embedded in the walls of downtown constructions, though they are nowadays highlighted as a source of distinction.

Giuseppe succeeded in building the mill. Nearing thirty and feeling his career well underway, he began to think of marriage. There were few family contacts to draw upon and Tivoli was a small town with almost no Jews, so he needed to look elsewhere. Through business dealings he met Guido Treves, a young Jewish lawyer from Florence who was making a name for himself negotiating commercial transactions and would go on to head a major insurance company. He introduced Giuseppe to his younger sister Amelia, an attractive young woman who was clearly from a good family.

Giuseppe Segrè and Amelia Treves were married in July of 1889 and settled in Tivoli. Like many young Italian Jews at the time, the newlyweds retained their Jewish identity in a cultural sense but were otherwise non-observant except for a small number of traditions. In any case, Tivoli had no synagogue. Two years after their marriage my father was born; he was named Angelo for his paternal grandfather, the Bozzolo merchant. Two years later another boy, Marco, was born, named after his maternal grandfather, and little more than a dozen years later a third, Emilio, came along. All three of them remembered growing up in an idyllic setting of Roman ruins, Renaissance villas, and magnificent views of a countryside that stretched all the way to Rome.

By the time of World War I, travel back and forth from Rome to Tivoli was easy and convenient, so Giuseppe decided to move his family and the paper mill's commercial headquarters to the nearby metropolis. His brother Claudio, living at that time in a beautiful apartment near Piazza Navona, the center of the city's old Baroque section, alerted him to an attractive housing possibility.

He had heard that an aging cardinal was vacating an apartment on the floor below his, and the empty apartment was like his own but larger. Giuseppe acted quickly and became his older brother's neighbor. For the next ten years, until his death, Claudio's three nephews came to regard him almost as a second father. When they in turn married and had children, each of my two uncles named a son Claudio. By the time I was born, there were already two young Claudios in the family, so my parents decided to name me after Gino, my father's younger brother. However, they gave me Claudio as a middle name.

Gino, the last of Angelo and Egle's three sons, was born in 1864. Like Claudio, but even more studious, he too attended Pavia's *Collegio Ghislieri* and then set out on an academic career in Italy's nationalized university system. His primary interest was Roman law, a subject that was then and still is the basis of Italy's legal system.* As his eminence in that field and other areas of the law grew, he was often called to consult on difficult cases, but research and teaching remained his focus. In his younger years he taught at less prominent Italian universities, but, rising in the ranks as his work became better known, he was soon made a professor in Turin. Finding that city much to his liking, he turned down offers of a professorship in the even more prestigious Rome.** Like Claudio, Gino became a member of the *Accademia dei Lincei.*

Advising the government on legal matters or academic questions of national importance often brought him to Rome, and he almost always stayed with his brothers. My father remembered how the three of them would reminisce about Bozzolo when they gathered, often switching back to speaking the Lombard dialect of their childhood.

None of the three Segrè brothers was an observant Jew, but they continued to think of themselves as members of that larger Italian Jewish community and they chose Jewish women as partners. However, by the time their own children married, this expectation had broken down. My father married out of the faith, as did his uncle Gino's daughters. The oldest did marry

*Unlike in the Anglo-Saxon case-based system of jurisprudence, Roman law is foundational in Italian legal studies and one or more courses on the subject are required to obtain a law degree at an Italian university.
** Much beloved in Turin, there is now a high school in the city named after him, the *Liceo Scientifico Gino Segrè.*

an Italian Jew, but the second married a non-observant Italian Catholic, and the third a Swiss Protestant.

Gino died in 1942, the year before the Germans took control of North-Central Italy. His widow and middle daughter survived the war by going into hiding near Turin. The youngest daughter was safe in Switzerland, but the oldest, Egle, her husband Edgardo Levi, and their two children, Enzo and Eva, were caught by the Nazis while trying to make their way to refuge in Switzerland. Deported to Auschwitz, only Enzo, by then in his early twenties, survived the ordeal. I met him in Turin after the war, but I was just a child and remember little of our encounter. All I really know about his postwar life is that after a few years in Turin he committed suicide. One did not talk about it. This all happened before the appearance of Primo Levi's books brought discussions of life in the camps into the open. Did Enzo Levi and Primo Levi, not related as far as I know, but both young Levis from Turin, meet in Auschwitz or afterwards? It seems very likely. What might they have said to one another? Perhaps Enzo just wanted to forget, but it hardly seems a coincidence that both Enzo and Primo committed suicide.

CHAPTER 19

The Tuscan Great Grandparents

THE LIVES of my Segrè great-grandparents seem serene when one thinks of all the changes and turmoil they witnessed. They lived most of their lives in a town too small to warrant a ghetto, never traveled very far, and their children all did well. On growing older, they left Bozzolo to be near their son Claudio and died there at peace.

The lives of my other two Italian Jewish great-grandparents were more complicated. Their story shows many interesting facets of how Italian Jews were accepted in the larger Christian society, but it also illustrates some of the tension they experienced while trying to move forward.

By the 1830s, ghetto life in Italy's larger cities had a porous quality. It was becoming possible to escape the ghetto confines, increasingly so as the years passed, and more noticeably as one moved further north in Italy. Jewish life in Florence is a good example of the changing picture. Under pressure from Pope Paul IV, the city had introduced a ghetto in 1570 and the Jews from neighboring towns were brought to Florence and enclosed within its walls. The ghetto was not formally abolished until 1848 but the requirement for Jews to live within its boundaries had been abandoned several decades earlier. This occurred mainly because the ruling Archdukes of Tuscany were Habsburg cousins and had adopted the Austrian Empire's more liberal attitude toward Jews. Florentine Jews who could afford to do so largely moved out of the ghetto at this time, leaving behind them a poor and highly congested neighborhood.

As a result, the city's Jews increasingly saw having to live in the ghetto as a matter of finances.

Though not born in Florence, this is where Marco Treves, my other great-grandfather, began his career and where he had most of his success. He was an architect who worked on both Jewish and Catholic projects, but his best-known undertaking was the design of the city's grand synagogue.

He first came to Florence in 1834. Born twenty years earlier in Vercelli, one of the Piedmontese towns big enough to already have a sizeable Jewish population in 1600, he was the sixteenth and last child of Jacob Treves and Allegra Olivetti.* After attending the local school for young Jews, he went to work for a much older brother who was a silversmith. In the early nineteenth century this was a prized profession because gold and silver were one of the few ways Jews could store accumulated wealth; it was only recently that they had been allowed to purchase land, and previously they had often not even able to own their own house.

Having shown skill in drawing, design, and sculpting, Marco considered a career in the arts. He wasn't sure what that would entail but decided to move to Florence, a city known for its beauty, its tolerance of Jews, and, importantly for him, its highly regarded art school, the *Accademia delle Belle Arti*. Succeeding in gaining entrance, he managed to do very well in his studies and graduate with a degree in architecture.

Feeling young and adventurous, he then moved to Rome instead of staying in Florence; there would be time later for settling down. A small but noticeable easing in dealings with Jews had begun to take place even in Rome, so Marco Treves did not have much difficulty finding employment in a Roman

* Perhaps his mother was related to the Olivettis of typewriter fame, another Piedmontese Jewish family. Given the relatively small size of the Piedmontese Jewish community, such distant connections are common.

architectural studio. He also managed to earn some extra income by selling watercolor illustrations of Roman scenes for publication in tourist books. Did he live in the ghetto, then four thousand strong, and did he wear clothing meant to mark him as a Jew? I don't think so, but I do know that he remained very observant and went to the ghetto for synagogue services.

After three years of piecemeal work in Rome, Marco concluded it was time to look for something more stable. He chose to return to Florence, which was more welcoming to Jews than Rome. He quickly obtained a promising position as an architect, and within a year he married Elisa Basevi, a young woman from a prosperous local Jewish family. All was going well, but two years later, as she was preparing to give birth to their first child, Elisa contracted typhoid fever. The baby only lived for two days after being born, and Elisa died two weeks later. Disconsolate, Marco Treves buried them side by side and returned to Vercelli. The constant reminders of his lost happiness made life in Florence intolerable.

Three years passed. Recovered from the dual blows of losing his wife and child, and eager to restart his career, Marco traveled to London to see a new building he had heard talked about, the Great Exhibition of the Works of Industry of All Nations, better known simply as the Crystal Palace. Invigorated, Marco decided to stop in Paris to see French friends from his years in Rome. Marco had met these friends when they were living in Rome as winners of the Prix de Rome competition, a three-to-five-year fellowship the French Government awarded to promising young painters, sculptors, and architects. Marco's friendship with these talented young men had come about quite naturally, for they were all about his age and were mostly architects with interests much like his own. The connection was made easier because, having grown up in a Piedmont still under French influence, Marco was fluent in French.

His old friends encouraged him to stay in Paris, claiming it would be a great boost for his career even if he should later choose to return to Italy. One of them, Hector Lefuel, was overseeing several big projects, including extending the Palais de Louvre and working on the Palais de Tuileries. He offered Marco a job on the spot and Marco accepted.

He remained in Paris for the next five years, but increasingly found himself missing Italy. Now past forty, he began thinking of going back there and perhaps even remarrying. He still had friends in Florence and, on a trip there, one of them introduced him to Elisa Orvieto, the daughter of a Florentine Jewish family that was deeply rooted in the city's community. She was only twenty-two, nearly twenty years his junior, but marriages with such large age differences were not then uncommon. He thought she was pretty and charming. She thought he was proper, dignified, and very nice. In addition, she was confident that they would eventually settle in Florence, which would mean she would not have to live apart from her friends and family. Marco proposed marriage and Elisa accepted.

Marco and Elisa's first year as a married couple was spent in Paris while he concluded his commitments there, but she and her parents were eager to have them return to Florence. Marco also felt this might be the right time to restart his career there, particularly now that he had the cachet of having been an architect in Paris, the world leader of style.

The newlyweds planned to live in the center of Florence but knew they would also have access to the beautiful sixteenth-century country villa Elisa's parents had acquired twenty years earlier, in the late 1830s. At the time, they, along with some of their cousins, were almost certainly the first Jews to purchase such storied residences. They had done so warily, renting for a few years to see if they would be welcomed by their non-Jewish neighbors; reassured, they had happily gone ahead with the acquisition. Their villa did not have a view of nearby Florence but, surrounded by beautiful gardens and cultivated fields, living in it felt like being in open countryside. Yet they were only a mile away from *Porta Romana,* the old city door on the southern road that led to Rome. This made the villa close enough to reach, even on days when Talmudic law forbade greater travel.

CHAPTER 20

The Florence Synagogue

In preparation for Marco and Elisa's return to Florence, her parents rented a spacious apartment for them in a small square near Santa Maria del Fiore, the church almost always simply known as the Duomo. In quick succession, Elisa gave birth to four children, one every other year: Giuseppina, Jacopo, Paolina, and Guido. By then, their apartment no longer felt spacious. A fifth child, my grandmother Amelia, was born after they moved nearby to a larger apartment on the *piano nobile* of an old *palazzo* in Piazza San Lorenzo.

Meanwhile, Marco's career was advancing in both private and public arenas. During his first years back in the city, the biggest architectural project afoot was a new façade for Santa Croce, the Franciscan order's magnificent church. The church's origins dated back to the late thirteenth century and the façade had remained unchanged, still the original rough stone. Various proposals had been made over the centuries for decorating it, but nothing had been accomplished. In the meantime, the Basilica had become known for its frescos by Giotto, its sculptures by Donatello and Della Robbia, and as the burial place of many of the greatest Florentines, including Michelangelo, Machiavelli, and Galileo. Santa Croce was one of Florence's gems, and the inability to decorate it with a suitable façade was embarrassing.

In the late 1830s, a proposal by the architect Niccolò Matas, a young professor at Florence's *Accademia delle Belle Arti,* was tentatively accepted; yet it still took until 1857 for construction to begin. Surprisingly, as Marco Treves noted, Matas was a Jew.

The façade was considered attractive, but some Florentines remained uneasy about the architect being a Jew, going so far as to make the unlikely assumption that the six-pointed star he had decoratively placed at the top of the façade was a Star of David.

Nevertheless, the choice of Matas to design Santa Croce's facade reassured Marco Treves that he need not worry about entering the biggest Florentine architectural competition in a long time: a new façade for the Duomo.

Topped by Brunelleschi's magnificent cupola, the Duomo is Florence's central church. It too had a bare façade. For reasons that remain unclear, the early one had been completely dismantled in 1587, its marble pieces broken up, its statues removed and the whole replaced by simple brick. The original plan was to cover it with frescoes, but that was soon dismissed and, amid swirling controversies about how best to proceed, the façade had remained untouched for almost three centuries.

There were more than forty entries when the design competition was announced in 1861. Three, including one by Marco Treves and associates, were considered particularly meritorious, but no final decision was made. The competition was renewed in 1864 and again in 1865, at which time a winner was finally announced; Treves and associates were the runners-up.

Marco was disappointed by the outcome but had not lacked for interesting projects in the meantime, many relating to his being Jewish. Early Italian synagogues were hidden away in their city's ghetto, unmarked on the outside to avoid vandalism, but now that Jews were seemingly accepted, every major Italian Jewish community wanted a new synagogue—or rather, a new Israelite Temple, as they were now called. At the very least, they wanted to have their old synagogue refashioned and modernized.

Florence's Jewish community was no exception in its wish for a grand Israelite Temple. Its members wanted it to be built far from the old ghetto, preferably in one of the city's new fashionable sections. There were many such districts because Florence had grown rapidly after political negotiations led the new Kingdom of Italy to move its capital from Turin to Florence in 1865. Marco Treves had even been the architect in charge of building a major triumphal arch to mark King Victor Emanuel II's entry into the city that year.

However, the Jewish community had not been able to gather the funds to build a new Israelite Temple. That changed in 1870 when David Levi, the wealthy president of the Florence Jewish community, died, bequeathing his entire estate of close to one and a half million lire for the project. A design competition was quickly held; it was won by Marco Treves, in collaboration with Mariano Falcini and Vincente Micheli, two Catholic architects.

MARCO TREVES—FAMILY PHOTO

Marco Treves' dream was coming true. Nearing sixty, with a stately manner, a piercing gaze, and a flowing beard, he looked very much like a prophet of old. The temple would be his greatest project, his legacy, the combining of his deep religious faith with all the skills he had acquired during his career. Its scale would match that of the largest of the city's churches, other than the truly monumental Duomo, for it would have to be able to seat the almost two thousand individuals of the city's Jewish population. But it was also important that the temple did not look like a Catholic church. The chosen design accomplished this by modeling itself on Istanbul's great mosque, *Haghia Sophia.* This was a familiar move: large Jewish communities throughout Europe were adopting the Moorish Revival style, their answer to the contemporary Neo-Gothic one adopted by Christian churches.

Inaugurated in 1882, the Israelite Temple was deemed a great success by the city's Jews. Other major cities in Italy soon followed Florence's lead in building grand new synagogues: Milan's was completed in 1892, and Rome's was inaugurated in a 1904 ceremony attended by King Victor Emanuel III. But Florence's was commonly thought to be the most beautiful and has been an acknowledged model in the construction of other synagogues world-wide.

Marco Treves' last major design project was a new Jewish cemetery for Florence. The old one, built when it was forbidden for Jews to be buried within city limits, had been located just outside the city's walls, but their demolition and the subsequent city expansion meant a new cemetery was needed. After it was completed and the old grave markers moved, it was ready for its designer to be buried in an honored spot.

Building a new Israelite Temple was a major step in revitalizing Florence's Jewish community, but its members felt more needed to be done. Enthusiastic support for the fight for Italian unification and the resulting possibilities for complete assimilation had shaken the old forms of observance and the new generation was finding them difficult to maintain.

Silvia Vidale, a first cousin of my father's and like him a grandchild of Marco Treves, has written an elegiac family memoir of growing up surrounded by the elders of her interrelated

The Synagogue of Florence (1894) by Giuseppe Barberis.
PUBLIC DOMAIN, VIA WIKIMEDIA COMMONS.

Florence Jewish families, but she does not shrink from pointing out some of the difficulties that came with that upbringing. Born the same year as my father, 1891, she describes how her generation had not been able to follow the old ways of religious observance and was uncertain about how to go forward. Her writing on the subject echoes, in a more graceful way, some of Rachele Moncalvo's opinions in the Castelnuovo novel, *I Moncalvo.*

> I can say that in that very religious atmosphere, I learned very little about religion except for the sense of belonging to something solemn, exclusive, a little mysterious (and secretly uncomfortable) that separated us from others, the ones who went to Mass on Sundays: the servants, the farmers and, more widely, from all those within eyesight, a vista that stretched to a far horizon.

I quoted in the prologue what she wrote about her grandparents and other ancestors:

> Faith, for the old ones, was comfort, union, sustenance, and it filled every hour of the day. They had absorbed it, breathing it in during their youth like the very air, and their whole lives had been filled by it, but in a world around them that had changed, they had not been able to teach it even to their children.

The members of the Florence Jewish community were aware of needing a leader to help them deal with the changing face of Italian Judaism, but what kind of rabbi did this require? Who would make best use of the new Temple? These were the challenges for the community, and they cast a wide net in their search, even looking beyond Italy's borders. Their final choice, made in 1890, was a surprise: thirty-two-year-old Samuel Hirsch Margulies, born in Berezhany, a city in present-day Ukraine, a graduate of the Breslau Jewish Theological Seminary, a former student at the Universities of Breslau and Leipzig, and a former rabbi in Hamburg.

CHAPTER 21

Italian Zionism: Jewish or Italian?

LEARNED, ENERGETIC, and charismatic, Samuel Margulies more than lived up to Florence's expectations. He became a force in Italian Judaism and made sure his influence would continue by founding a seminary that trained many new rabbis, the *Collegio Rabbinico Italiano*. He also inaugurated and then edited the *Rivista Israelitica*, a scholarly journal that centered on Italian Jewish history and culture.

But Margulies soon found himself embroiled in a set of problems that transcended borders. While Italian Jews were thriving, *pogroms* began violently shaking the Pale of Settlement in the wake of Tsar Alexander II's 1881 assassination. Terror shook Jews in cities such as Warsaw, Kyiv, Odessa, and in countryside *shtetls*.

Western Jews felt sympathy for the suffering their brethren were undergoing. They understood why these Jews were seeking safe havens in the West, but many were wary of welcoming in their midst Jews they felt were so unlike themselves. They were also reluctant to have their loyalty to Judaism appear greater than their loyalty to their nation. This sentiment was widely true in Italy, the country seemingly most free of anti-Semitism. Rabbi Margulies' position was ambiguous for, although he was happily settled in Florence, he was also one of *them*; born and raised in Ukraine, he was an Eastern Jew. He watched closely as the crisis mounted and the flow from the East gathered momentum.

Thoughts of a new homeland for Jews were beginning to emerge. Going forward with this notion, Jews found a leader in Theodore Herzl. In February of 1896 he had published *Der Judenstaat* (The Jewish State), which became the foundational book of modern Zionism; it called for Jews to leave Europe and to create their own homeland in Palestine. Meeting with passionate acclaim in some quarters and passionate condemnation in others, news of the book spread quickly through the Jewish world.

An International Zionist Congress convened for the first time in August of 1897. Many Italian Jews watched its conclusions from afar. Though humanitarian and philanthropic aid to other Jews seemed desirable, the suggestion of mixed loyalties was not widely welcome in Italy. The novelist Enrico Castelnuovo put the matter succinctly in a letter he wrote to the fledgling Venetian Zionist group "I was born a Jew, and I shall remain a Jew, but no one will force me to go to Jerusalem with the Chosen People. I am Italian and I do not understand what is meant by Jewish Nationality. These are my ideas on Zionism." But not all Italian Jews held those views, and a *Federazione Sionistica* supporting Zionism was soon founded.

Although no Italian Jew had officially attended the first Zionist Congress, a few went to the later ones. After the 1903 session, Theodore Herzl asked the by-then very well-known Margulies, who had given a strong speech in support of him, to arrange a meeting for him with Italy's king. Acceding to the request, Margulies consulted Victor Emanuel III, and an invitation to the Zionist leader was soon forthcoming; a late January 1904 date was set for the encounter. There were many reasons why Herzl wanted a meeting with Italy's king. He knew it would raise the profile of Zionism in Italy, and it would encourage the country's Jews to join the movement.

Herzl arrived in Rome at the predetermined time. The city's Jewish community had been growing rapidly and it was playing an important role in the city becoming a financial and cultural center. The old unsanitary ghetto buildings had been torn down, replaced by ones protected from the Tiber's flooding by newly erected bulwarks. That city section was becoming an attractive neighborhood and was about to add an imposing new synagogue, a structure that would be visible from all over Rome.

Three days after his session with Victor Emanuel III, Herzl also met with Pope Pius X. The city's Jews treated Herzl's visit as a mark of how far they had come, but they were still unsure of which Jews he should meet with while in Rome. Margulies removed Luzzatti from the initial list of prospective contacts even though, as Italy's Minister of Finance at the time, he was Italy's most prominent Jew in government. Margulies did this, as he told Herzl, because, "*Egli appartiene ai più fanatici assimilinazionisti*" ("He belongs to the most fanatical assimilationists").

Herzl's visit did give a great boost to the *Federazione Sionistica,* but it was short-lived. Dissension began quickly as the divide widened between those who believed the movement's main thrust should be philanthropic and those who thought it should be political. The final straw came in 1911. While Zionist organizations were negotiating with Turkey over land in Palestine, an unrelated dispute over the possession of Libya turned into a full-fledged war between Italy and Turkey. What had been a difficult situation for Italian Zionism now became an impossible one.

This landscape changed with the collapse of the Ottoman Empire. In 1916, anticipating the Empire's demise, the British and the French Governments signed the Sykes-Picot Agreement, partitioning the Middle East into British and French mandates, with Palestine falling in the British zone. Two years later, on November 2, 1917, the United Kingdom's Foreign Secretary, Lord Balfour, issued the Balfour Declaration, a statement originally appearing in a letter he wrote to Lord Rothschild, a leader of the British Jewish community. It announced that the British Government viewed with favor the establishment in Palestine of a homeland for Jews, provided it did not prejudice the civil and religious rites of existing non-Jewish communities already there.

Even Italian assimilationists could support this declaration. They made that clear during a large demonstration organized by Pro-Israel, an association of non-Jewish Zionist sympathizers. Held in Rome at the Teatro Nazionale on December 8, 1918, the demonstration brought together many prominent figures in Italian Judaism, including Luzzatti. They all praised a document summarizing the proceedings, the contents of which were essentially the same as those of the Balfour Declaration.

CHAPTER 22

The Grand Lady of Italian Socialism

THE RISE of Zionism in the late nineteenth and early twentieth centuries affected Jews but meant very little to the average Italian. However, another movement was simultaneously emerging that would matter to all Italians and in which Jews would play a prominent role: socialism. One woman, a former anarchist, was central to its founding and subsequent development in Italy. Her name was Anna Kuliscioff.

She was born Anja Moiseeva Rosenstejn in 1854, the oldest

ANNA KULISCIOFF IN FLORENCE (1908) BY MARIO NUNES VAIS.
PUBLIC DOMAIN, VIA WIKIMEDIA COMMONS

daughter in a wealthy Jewish Crimean merchant family. Brilliant and beautiful, she went abroad at seventeen because she was determined to attend university, and at that time Russia did not offer higher education to women. After two years in Switzerland, she was recalled to Russia by a Tsarist decree. Having been radicalized during those two years, Anna joined a group of anarchist revolutionaries when she returned. A year later she married Pëter Makarevič, a young fellow conspirator. Arrested for his political activities, he was condemned to hard labor and died in prison soon afterwards.

Meanwhile, on the run after being charged with stoking an uprising, Anna changed her surname to Kuliscioff, a common Russian name given to the unwanted. After leaving her homeland for good at twenty-three, she arrived in Paris and there began a passionate but troubled relationship with Andrea Costa, an Italian anarchist. Over the next years they led a peripatetic existence between Switzerland, France, and Italy, with frequent separations caused by one or the other and sometimes both being in prison.

In Italy, having contracted tuberculosis during a fifteen-month term she served in a Florence jail, Kuliscioff decided living in a more moderate climate would be advisable. She moved to Naples with her daughter Andreina, born to her and Costa two years earlier. Kuliscioff, who by then had broken off her relationship with Costa, now chose to concentrate on the medical studies she had begun while in Switzerland. Specializing in gynecology with an avowed aim of treating indigent women, she became the first woman to graduate from Naples' university with a medical degree.

During her years in Naples, Kuliscioff slowly found her political ideas evolving away from anarchism toward a Marxist view of society and from there to a belief in reform through education and organization for welfare. She also met Filippo Turati. He, trained as a lawyer, had been working in Naples on a pioneering study linking crime to underlying social conditions. Born near Milan, he was, like her, thirty years old. They fell in love and remained together until her death forty years later, though they never married. Their union was a deep one, a meeting of mind and soul.

Kuliscioff moved to Milan to be with Turati, and her Piazza Duomo apartment became the central headquarters of the city's growing socialist movement. To provide it with an intellectual underpinning, Kuliscioff and Turati took over the direction of the left-wing magazine, *Critica Sociale* (Social Criticism). The first issue they put out, edited in her apartment's living room, appeared in January of 1891 and rapidly gained a wide, interested readership. Kuliscioff and Turati were recognized as the movement's leading intellectuals and the magazine became the critical organ through which they broadcast their own agenda as well as spreading others' ideas.

Turati became a city councilor and as such represented Milan at a national meeting of groups attempting to organize a united left-wing front. The majority of the assembled decided to split off from the anarchists in their midst, and proceeded to establish the *Partito dei Lavoratori Italiani* (Italian Workers' Party), a party that a year later changed its name to *Partito Socialista Italiano* (Italian Socialist Party).

The Italian Socialist movement rapidly gained adherents. Its representation in the Chamber of Deputies, which now included Turati, increased from an initial four members in 1892 to sixteen in 1896, the rise marking a growing resistance to the rightward swing of government policies. Unhappiness with both cabinet and monarch came to a head in 1898 in protests about increases in the price of bread, the main standard fare for the poor. Demonstrations in several Italian cities culminated on the seventh of May with sixty thousand Milanese workers going on strike and setting out on a march toward the city center. Aware of what had been planned, the government had stationed forty-five thousand soldiers in Milan, ordering them to stop the marchers at any cost. The soldiers opened fire on them, killing eighty marchers by their own estimate; the opposition claimed the number was far higher.

King Umberto I's response was to award the Great Cross of the Order of Savoy to Fiorenzo Bava Beccaria, the general in charge, thanking him also for presiding over a subsequent trial during which fifteen hundred protestors were imprisoned. Two years later, the king was killed by bullets from an Italian American anarchist who claimed he committed the act to revenge the workers who had died in Milan.*

Even though they had worked toward a peaceful settlement of the disputes, both Kuliscioff and Turati were arrested, and publication of *Critica Sociale* banned. Kuliscioff was soon released, but Turati was sentenced to twelve years in prison for his supposed role in the protests. However, he was amnestied a year later and allowed to return to his post in the Chamber of Deputies.

Italy's growing social unrest at the beginning of the new century was forcing the country to start edging toward a more progressive agenda. Kuliscioff, the unquestioned feminist leader in Italian Socialism believed the time might now be ripe for action on this front. She had argued in her 1890 book, *The Monopoly of Man*, that women were exploited in both the workplace and the home, further maintaining that socialism's efforts to remedy these inequalities needed to be a central focus of the movement's mission. Therefore, she and Turati now prepared a measure dealing with working conditions for women and children. It stipulated that the minimum working age for children be raised from nine to twelve and the maximum working day for women be set at twelve hours. A maternity leave of four weeks, the first ever, was also included in the bill. Turati introduced it in Parliament, and in 1902 it passed into law.

*A year after Umberto I's death, another anarchist, Leon Czolgosz, assassinated United States President William McKinley. Czolgosz was reportedly inspired by the earlier assassination.

Kuliscioff and Turati were hopeful that further measures would be put forward by a united socialist movement, but action was made more difficult by a fissure that began to appear in the Socialist Party in the early twentieth century. Some favored a more gradual transformation through parliamentary reform and others adopted a revolutionary stance: reformists versus maximalists. In the years to come, this split would have dire consequences. Many believe Socialism's inability to present a united front was one of the principal factors that allowed Fascism to gain control of Italy.

The divide between the reformists and maximalists wasn't the only split in early twentieth-century Italian left-wing politics. In the past, Kuliscioff and Turati had always agreed on political strategy, but a 1911 electoral bill caused a serious difference of opinion between them, as they openly acknowledged in an exchange that they published in the *Critica Sociale.* The bill centered on the possibility of obtaining universal male suffrage, a topic then being debated in Parliament. Turati felt that also pushing for women's suffrage would endanger the chance of obtaining a more limited victory, but Kuliscioff said this was too calculating. She maintained the party needed the influx of women and the energy it would create.

The law passed in the form Turati supported. Kuliscioff was incensed, her anger exacerbated by seeing ballots that had to be prepared with pictures indicating party affiliation because literacy was no longer a requirement for voting. Weren't literate women more capable of making political decisions than illiterate men? To continue the fight, she founded a new weekly journal, *La Difesa delle Lavoratrici* (*The Defense of Women Workers*). Its first issue appeared in January 1912.

It would take more than thirty years for Italian women to obtain the right to vote and forty years before they would be able to run for a seat in Parliament!

CHAPTER 23

Dueling Socialists: Mussolini and Treves

THE EARLY-twentieth-century struggle between reformists and maximalists for control of Italy's Socialist Party seemed to have been settled in favor of the former. This approach was strengthened when a young man Kuliscioff and Turati had welcomed as a leader of their wing of the Socialist Party returnaed to Milan. They had first met Claudio Treves* when he was a twenty-three-year-old Jewish graduate of Turin's law school interested in talking to them. Writing for the *Critica* had been the beginning of his stellar career as a reporter and essayist. He had then gone on to travel throughout Europe as correspondent for foreign newspapers, always hoping to come back to Milan and team up with his mentors. Now he was back, eventually entering Parliament as a deputy in the Chamber and taking on the role of Editor-in-Chief of *Avanti*, the Socialist Party's official daily newspaper.

Matters seemed to be going well for the Italian Socialism movement, but Italy's 1911 decision to gain control of Libya by starting a war against Turkey caused a new crisis. The internal conflict came to a head at the party's annual meeting, when Chamber of Deputies Socialist Party members Ivanoe Bonomi and Leonida Bissolati announced they supported the war, an action contrary to the party stance that war was an evil conse-

*Claudio Treves is probably related at least distantly to my great-grandfather, Marco Treves, since they trace their roots to adjoining small Piedmontese towns. Claudio Treves's son Paolo became, like his father, an editor of the Socialist newspaper *Avanti* and then a member of Parliament.

quence of capitalism. After being ferociously attacked by maximalists and then expelled from the party, the two formed their own party, which they called the Italian Socialist Reform Party.

Turati and Treves had been guiding the center of the reformist wing of the Socialist Party in the Chamber, but with Bissolati and Bonomi gone, they were increasingly viewed as the conservative wing and criticized as such. The party's directorate was again moving to the left, a swing marked by Treves being dismissed as editor of the party's newspaper.

At this delicate juncture Turati and Treves were joined in the Chamber of Deputies by a like-minded forty-year-old lawyer, Giuseppe Emanuele Modigliani,* another of those remarkable Jews from Livorno. He would turn out to be a great help to the reformists.

The maximalist attack on them was led by an unscrupulous twenty-nine-year-old fiery orator who was attending the party convention for the first time. His name was Benito Mussolini. The future dictator was born in Romagna, a region of North-Central Italy near Bologna, his mother a devout Catholic and his father an avowed socialist. To satisfy both he had been baptized in the Church but also given the names Benito Andrea as homages to Benito Juarez, Mexico's nationalist leader, and the anarchist Andrea Costa, Anna Kuliscioff's former lover.

Born in 1883, Mussolini emigrated to Switzerland in 1902 to avoid compulsory military service. While there he attended lectures at the University of Lausanne and lived by what he could earn in manual labor. Angry and self-important, he developed an aggrandized view of himself as both an intellectual and as predestined for greatness. Coming back to Italy, Mussolini found work as a reporter and began to enter left wing politics. In 1911, he saw that taking a hard line on the government's war

*He was an older brother of the painter Amadeo Modigliani, who moved to Paris in 1906 and died there in 1920, only becoming famous years later. Giuseppe Emanuele Modigliani fled to Paris to escape Fascist imprisonment later in the 1920s.

in Libya might be the vehicle for him to raise his Socialist Party profile. Doing so led to his being chosen to direct the party's newspaper, edited until recently by Treves. His inflammatory writing and calls for revolution led to a marked increase in readership, for which he was widely praised. Following Mussolini's line, the party now went on to emphasize ideological purity. Allegiance with other groups on common electoral aims became unacceptable, and freemasonry or similar affiliations were deemed incompatible with party membership.

Feeling that the time was ripe for further strengthening his control over the party, Mussolini renewed his attacks on Turati, Treves, Modigliani, and other members of the reformist center. In early 1914 he told Treves, still a contributor to *Avanti,* that his services were no longer needed at the paper.

But the balance of power between maximalists and reformists shifted again at the start of World War I. In July of 1914 Mussolini published an editorial entitled "*Abbasso la Guerra*" ("Down With War"), maintaining that a conflict would only help capitalist causes, but in October he switched to supporting the war, asserting that the nation's population, once fully armed, could overthrow bourgeois powers.

Since "No adherence, no sabotage," had been adopted as the Socialist Party's official policy, its members began to suspect Mussolini of playing a complicated double game. This seemed to be confirmed when he resigned from his post at *Avanti.* Within weeks, Mussolini accepted the leadership of the questionably funded *Il Popolo d'Italia,* a new paper eventually associated with the emerging Fascist Party. This led, on November 24, 1914, to his being expelled from the Socialist Party.

Mussolini developed an increasing animosity toward the Socialist Party's reformists, with special venom directed at Treves. In March of 1915 he wrote a particularly vicious set of articles in his newspaper, claiming that Treves' populist beliefs were postures and that he was a cynic living off his wife's wealth. Treves' wife, Venetian-born Olga Levi, was indeed wealthy, but

Treves was careful to live by his work as an attorney and as a Parliamentarian. Adding to the hypocrisy, Mussolini had himself been conducting an affair with another Venetian-born Jewish woman who was helping finance his career.* She was even richer than Treves' wife.

Despite party injunctions against dueling, Treves rose to the bait and challenged the considerably younger Mussolini to a duel, the weapon of choice being sabers. They met with their seconds on October 29, 1915, in a vacant house on Milan's periphery. Over the course of twenty-five minutes, eight rounds were fought. Both suffered wounds, Treves' more serious than Mussolini's. They parted ways without either one making a move toward reconciliation. This was the last time they met.

After hearing of the duel, Modigliani sent Treves a telegram that, loosely translated, read, "I disapprove, I would have done the same, I salute you."

*Margherita Sarfatti was a well-known art critic and collector. Year later, when she was no longer his mistress, she wrote a hagiographic biography of Mussolini entitled *Dux.* Translated into eighteen languages, it became an influential piece of propaganda in the 1920s.

CHAPTER 24

The Great War

By the time Mussolini and Treves dueled, Italy was in a war that was strongly supported by the one and strongly opposed by the other. It was also without the allies it had chosen to unite with in case of war thirty years earlier. In May of 1882, abandoning previous pretenses of neutrality, Italy had joined the mutual defense agreement that already existed between Austria and Germany—those being the simpler names given to the Austro-Hungarian Empire and to the confederation of states brought together by Prussia. Prussia, guided by Otto Bismarck, had been a natural partner at that time. Having it as an ally in a war against Austria in 1866 had allowed Italy to annex Venice, and Prussia's defeat of France in 1870 had paved the way for the Italian army to occupy Rome that September. But after the start of World War I in 1914, Italy began to wonder if being part of the Triple Alliance was still in its best interest.

Antonio Salandra was then Italy's prime minister. Not only was he inexperienced, but the country's situation was soon made even more troublesome by the sudden death of Italy's veteran Minister of Foreign Affairs, the Marquess of San Giuliano. Feeling the need for a competent and trusted aid, Salandra turned to Sidney Sonnino, whose cabinet he had served in during one of Sonnino's brief stints as prime minister.

In the late fall of 1914, Salandra and Sonnino began engaging in a risky double game. Without consulting the Chamber of Deputies, they entered secret discussions with the Triple Entente of Britain, France, and Russia, while at the same time they were negotiating with their Triple Alliance partners on what Italy might expect in return for entering the war by their side. Should Italy remain neutral? Or, if not, which side should it join? Who had a better chance of winning, and what might they offer Italy for joining them?

By spring of 1915, fearing fighting would soon be over, Salandra felt he needed to choose one side or the other, lest Italy come out of the war empty-handed; he opted for the Triple Entente. Referring to his policy as *sacro egoismo* (sacred egoism), he didn't even discuss the matter with the military before making the decision. Busily preparing to join the Triple Alliance, they were shocked by his decision.

The secret Treaty of London, obligating Italy to enter on the Entente's side, was concluded on April 26, 1915. The Chamber of Deputies members, previously uninformed and in large measure favoring neutrality, were stunned by the news but quickly concluded that opposing the *fait accompli* was likely to lead to greater trouble. When the Chamber met on May 20, the deputies gave the government full powers "in case of war" by a 407 to 74 vote. Italy declared war on the Alliance three days later.

Italians were soon swept up in a wave of enthusiasm. Some Italian Jews had misgivings about fighting Jews from other nations and some opposed war in general, but on the average they were as patriotic—if not more so—than other Italians. They knew Italy had exhibited greater acceptance and more avenues of advancement for them than other European countries had, and they were eager to prove that the faith the country had shown in their *Italianità* (Italianess) was fully warranted.

I could document here the total number of Jewish soldiers, Jewish generals, and Jewish medal winners, but suffice it to say that in each category they outstripped what would have been expected of them given their percentage of the total Italian population. Even rabbis played their part in the war effort. After receiving encouragement from the head of Rome's Jewish community, the city's Chief Rabbi organized and led a group of rabbis to tend to Jewish soldiers.

The son of Mussolini's mistress, Roberto Sarfatti, enlisted with a false birth certificate in 1915, having turned fifteen only two months earlier. His age was soon discovered, and he was sent home. Two years later he volunteered and was accepted in the *Alpini,* elite mountain troops. In January of 1918 he captured a machine gun station and took dozens of Austrian soldiers as prisoners. Returning quickly to the offensive, he received a bullet in the head. Sarfatti was posthumously awarded the Gold Medal, Italy's highest military decoration; he was the youngest soldier to be so decorated.

The war was not going well for Italy. In May of 1916, Austria, keen on punishing Italy for having betrayed the Triple Alliance, launched an attack that succeeded in pushing Italian troops almost down to the valley of the Po River that bisects Northern Italy. The Italians held the line there, but worse was still to come.

In October of 1917 an epic battle in the country's far northeast almost brought fighting to an end in Italy. The decisive encounter, described in Hemingway's *Farewell to Arms,* took place near the town of Caporetto. Seven hundred thousand Italian soldiers faced an Austrian army half its size but well-led and reinforced by crack German divisions. The resulting abject defeat put Italy on the verge of surrender. Over the course of three weeks following the battle, much of their equipment was abandoned, troops deserted, and almost three hundred thousand Italian soldiers were taken prisoner. What remained of the army retreated nearly a hundred miles, finally taking a stand at the Piave River of northeast Italy. By that point, the advancing Austro-German army's supply lines were stretched so thin that the Italian army finally managed to stop their onslaught.

There was more than enough blame to be shared. The Prime Minister resigned, and the Army Chief was replaced. Italy was in crisis, its citizens fearful and despondent. Sonnino's old friend Leopoldo Franchetti, already depressed, committed suicide apparently after hearing the news of Caporetto. Even

Treves, Turati, and other Socialists who had opposed entering the war in 1915, now felt that national unity was necessary, or all could be lost.

Under new leadership the Italians repelled a final Austrian attack at the Piave River in June of 1918. They regrouped and went on the offensive, launching an attack near the town of Vittorio Veneto in October. That battle concluded with an Italian victory on November 3. An armistice with Austria was reached a day later, and on November 11, Germany signed a similar agreement with its opponents. Although the formal ending did not come until the Treaty of Versailles, World War I was effectively over.

CHAPTER 25

The War's Aftermath

THE END of World War I was marked by three great empires (Austro-Hungarian, Ottoman, and Russian) coming to an end and a new power, the United States, emerging on the world scene. A new Prime Minister, Vittorio Emanuele Orlando, and Sonnino, still Minister of Foreign Affairs, negotiated the peace treaty on Italy's behalf. Neither acted very effectively, though Italy's less than stellar war record also made it difficult for the two men to be viewed as representing a major power. What's more, Italy did not help itself by continuing to insist that the 1915 treaty of London be used as basis for a peace settlement, not acknowledging that conditions had changed radically since then. The Russian Revolution and the fall of the tsar meant the Triple Entente no longer existed, and the United States had entered the war without agreeing to the London Treaty's conditions, and they were not inclined to do so after the fact.

Instead, the United States President, Woodrow Wilson, presented fourteen points that he said should be used as guidelines for a lasting peace. These included the establishment of a League of Nations and that no secret treaties or alliances take place in the future. In addition, one of his points was that borders between countries should be drawn according to the nationality of the inhabitants. This idea found a sympathetic response in many Italians but was totally at odds with Sonnino's insistence that the Adriatic Sea was Italian territory, and his denial of Slavic natives' claims to the region. When their proposal did not meet acceptance, Orlando and Sonnino expressed their displeasure by leaving the conference in the middle of negotiations. They had to hurry back two weeks later, for the other participants were proceeding happily without them.

In the end, Italy received both Trento and Trieste, the two cities it most wanted to acquire, and was granted the area of Tyrol from Trento to the Brenner Pass, despite this being a German-speaking region. This was more than what Italy might have expected. Nevertheless, being denied their claims on the contested coast of the Adriatic Sea continued to fester in the Italian psyche. It would have been far better for Orlando and Sonnino to focus on obtaining foreign aid in rebuilding, rather than concentrating on demands for additional territory on the Adriatic Sea.

Italians greeted the war's end with jubilation, but disappointment quickly settled in when they realized how little had been gained through all the pain they had suffered. Half a million Italians had lost their lives and a far larger number had been wounded; many army officers were dissatisfied with civilian life, and more than a hundred thousand former deserters were fearful of retribution.

The cost to the economy had been enormous, and the necessary rebuilding required the import of expensive raw materials. This caused the government's deficit to increase by leaps and bounds, with outlays far exceeding revenues. Inflation set in. Farmers conscripted into service had been promised they would be given land when they returned from the battlefield, and factory workers had expected higher wages and better working conditions. None of that came to pass. Italy was adrift politically and in very poor shape economically.

Trust in the parliamentary system that had governed Italy since the time of Cavour and the *Risorgimento* had been badly eroded by the shuffling of government cabinets, the seeming corruption of the political system, and the top-down decisions made without consultation. It was becoming clear to everybody that the old Italian tactic of *transformismo*, the forming of governments from either the left-center or right-center party wing with appropriate accommodations, was not working any more.

The country now entered what historians have called the 1919-1920 *biennio rosso* (red two years), a period of cascading industrial strikes and countryside unrest. Italy seemed ripe for a revolution, but it was unclear how that might start, in what shape it would appear, and who would lead it.

Amid this uproar, the November 1919 general elections took place and were filled with startling surprises. One surprise was the performance of the *Partito Popolare Italiano* (Italian Populist Party), a political party that had not existed a year earlier. Known as the PPI, it had been founded in January 1919 by Don Luigi Sturzo, a very able Catholic priest with strong socialist beliefs. Rapidly gaining adherents, the party gathered a little over twenty percent of the popular vote. Though not directly supporting the PPI, Pope Benedict XV had helped it by lifting the Pius IX Vatican injunction that forbade Catholics from participating in Italian governance.

Don Sturzo wasn't the only one to start a new party in 1919. The Italian word *fascio* has several meanings: it is commonly used to describe a sheaf or perhaps a bundle of a grain, but it can also denote a beam of light. When Mussolini and his supporters founded the *Fasci Italiani di Combattimento* in 1919, *fascio* acquired a new connotation, that of bound-together combatants. Fascism is now commonly used to indicate a totalitarian ultra-nationalist form of government led by a dictator. However, 1919's *Fasci* were little more than bands of disgruntled war veterans with a propensity for violence. Their showing in the elections that year was a complete failure. The party did not win a single seat in the Chamber of Deputies.

The Socialist Party provided the biggest surprise of the 1919 elections. Aided by support from the labor union movement, particularly strong in the industrial North, the party won 156 out of the 508 seats in the Chamber, more than thirty-two percent of the popular vote. This made it Italy's largest political party. Having achieved this much, the party would have become the dominating force in Italian politics had it not been riven by internal conflicts. Its factions could seemingly only agree on one thing, their opposition to capitalism.

Some socialists believed that nothing needed to be done because capitalism would eventually collapse under its own weight. The party's directorate maintained that such a demise would only happen in the wake of a revolution akin to the Russian one, and a smaller socialist group advocated complete abstention from government while preparing for the revolution. However, most of the party's representatives in the Chamber of Deputies were reformers, and they neither shared the belief that capitalism would eventually collapse under its own weight, nor did they think a revolution was needed.

In the meantime, three young former students from Turin's law school, Antonio Gramsci, Palmiro Togliatti, and Umberto Terracini (a Jew) had begun formulating a new approach to left-wing politics that was more in line with directives from Moscow, and in 1921 they founded Italy's Communist Party. It grew quickly, attracting a large fraction of the Socialist Party, and those who remained in the Socialist Party also shared many views with the communists. The newly constituted Socialist Party began to consider expelling members who believed that reform could take place through parliamentary action.

That expulsion took place in early October of 1922. Turati, Claudio Treves, Giuseppe Emanuele Modigliani, and a talented, charismatic newcomer to Parliament, Giacomo Matteotti, felt they had no choice but to form yet another left-wing party, the Partito Socialista Unitario (Unitary Socialist Party).

The Italian left, split into sections, was finding it impossible to develop a coherent plan of action, but the liberal right was also unable to unite except in its fear of a Russian-type revolution. Trying to regroup, it asked veteran Giovanni Giolitti to take the reins of government as he had done so often in the past

Knowing how hard it would be to form a united government with opposition from Catholics and Socialists, Giolitti turned to the *Fasci*, for support. They had organized themselves into the *Partito Nazionale Fascista* (National Fascist Party). It was not very strong politically, but its use of teams of thugs, a tactic known as *squadrismo* (*squadra* being the Italian word for team), was highly effective at intimidating opponents

Giolitti had made a bad mistake. In the next election the new Fascist Party won thirty-five seats in Italy's Chamber of Deputies, including one for Mussolini. It now had a veneer of legality, and many began to think this party might have the tools—violence in the form of *squadrismo*—for dealing with social unrest.

Mussolini joined Catholics and Socialists in turning on Giolitti. Recognizing his failure, Giolitti resigned; he was replaced by the ineffective Ivanoe Bonomi and, six months later, by the even less effective Luigi Facta. Alarmed by Fascist rowdyism and the authorities' seeming tacit approval of their actions, Socialists and Catholic PPI members joined forces in July of 1922 to force a vote of no confidence in the Facta government. Facta resigned, but when nobody else from the conventional liberal parties was willing to try forming a coalition, he was put back in place. At this point an association of labor unions called for a probably ill-considered general strike, hoping it would aid in stabilizing the government's response to the increasing lawlessness.

With Italy in chaos, Mussolini decided the moment had come for him to take control of the situation. Asserting that Fascists would restore order, his troops broke the strike in two days. Now receiving considerable financial support from industrial magnates eager to avoid a repeat of the *biennio rosso,* Mussolini saw momentum swinging his way.

CHAPTER 26

The Rise of Fascism

IN LATE OCTOBER of 1922 several thousand Fascists gathered in the city of Perugia to prepare for a March on Rome. Italians did not know whether this was meant to be a *coup d'état* or simply a demonstration, but it was clear that one way or another, Fascists wanted to take control of the government. Many Jews feared socialism more than Fascism and over two hundred them joined the Black Shirts—the name given the Fascists because of their distinctive apparel.

The Chamber of Deputies was in disarray, uncertain of what to do. The king could have resisted, and General Emanuele Pugliese, the man overseeing the Italian Army troops in Rome, assured the Minister of the Interior that he was prepared to block any Fascist attempt to take control of the city. But when the prime minister sought permission to mount this defense, the king refused to ratify the order. Victor Emanuel III chose instead to invite Mussolini, who had stayed behind in Milan instead of going on the march, to form a new government. The *Duce* arrived the next day to accept the offer and the Black Shirts, now in Rome, staged a victory march.

Many Italians were reassured that the new government would not be a dictatorship when they saw that, although Mussolini kept some key cabinet positions for himself, he chose the widely trusted General Armando Diaz as Minister of War. Socialists were less confident, but their voices were absent from the cabinet and even largely from the Chamber of Deputies, except for the members of Turati's newly constituted reformist party.

Modigliani, Treves, and Turati made their presences known during the debates that followed the takeover, but Giacomo Matteotti, first elected to the Chamber in 1921, was the party's chief spokesman. He fiercely condemned the Fascists time after time. In 1924, feeling the need to do more, he published a book entitled, *The Fascists Exposed; a Year of Fascist Domination.* It documented the acts of violence with which the Fascists had attacked all opposition. Continuing in his crusade, on the 30th of May, 1924, Matteotti gave a speech in the Chamber denouncing the elections of the previous month, claiming that the wide majority won by the Fascist Party was only due to their intimidation of opponents. Ten days later he was murdered.

When news of his assassination reached the Chamber, a group of deputies led by the Liberal Party's Giovanni Amendola marched out in protest. They felt a turning point had been reached and Mussolini's takeover of the Italian Government needed to be stopped. But powerful former prime ministers Giolitti, Orlando, and Salandra did not support their move nor was the king willing to take any action.

In the past, *squadristi* had destroyed the printing presses of newspapers that criticized their actions. Now, encouraged by the majority's passivity, the Fascists passed a law that essentially ended freedom of the press. Matters in Parliament reached a head in January of 1925. Mussolini, who had previously denied any knowledge of the Matteotti murder, announced that he was assuming full responsibility for the action. Declaring that Italy wanted peace and quiet, he went on to say, "I shall give it all these, if possible, with love, but, if necessary, by force."

Some hoped the king would call for a new government now that Mussolini had brazenly admitted his culpability in the Matteotti assassination, but the moment when he might have acted had passed. *Il Duce,* daring his opponents to unseat him, put the question to a vote. Only thirty-three ballots were cast against him in the Chamber. Within forty hours, Italy became a dictatorship. Independent parties, including Giolitti's Liberal

Party, were outlawed. The deputies who had abandoned the Chamber in protest were not allowed to return to their seats.

The tactic of intimidation through force, always the not-so-hidden part of the Fascist program, was now carried out openly. Anyone of consequence who overtly opposed the party knew he or she was likely to suffer beatings and destruction of property or, in the most extreme case, assassination. Amendola's death from injuries suffered after being clubbed by *squadristi* in mid-1925 was a clear early demonstration of the license the Fascists felt to attack whoever they wanted.

In reaction to these events, an anti-Fascist underground newspaper, Italy's first, began to be published in January of 1925. Called *Non Mollare* (this loosely translates as *Don't Give Up* or *Keep Resisting*), it was the work of a small Florentine group headed by a college professor, Gaetano Salvemini, and two of his students, the brothers Carlo and Nello Rosselli

Quickly gaining wide readership, *Non Mollare* enraged Fascist leaders by documenting Matteotti's murder, Amendola's beating, and similar attacks. The paper's editors maneuvered to avoid detection by never using the same printing press twice and by printing only at night, but Salvemini was betrayed by a typographer. Granted provisional freedom on a technicality while awaiting trial, he escaped to France and from there to the United States. He was fortunate to have done so, for in October several contributors to *Non Mollare* were murdered by the Fascists; it was clear that Salvemini was on their list. Carlo Rosselli suspended the publication.

Mussolini's opponents had a great deal to fear. The leaders of the Socialist and Communist Parties quickly realized they would be persecuted regardless of whether they cooperated. Even Don Sturzo, with assent from the Vatican, was forced into exile.

Giacinto Serrati, who had led the left wing of the Socialist Party into the Communist Party, died of a heart attack while on his way to a party meeting in the spring of 1926; his funeral was the Communist Party's last semi-public occasion. One of its leaders, Palmiro Togliatti, escaped being imprisoned because he happened to be in Moscow when the mandate for his arrest was issued. Its other leaders, Antonio Gramsci and Umberto Terracini, were less fortunate. Gramsci, already in poor health when he entered prison, died in 1937 without regaining his freedom. His wide-ranging *Prison Notebooks,* smuggled out from his cell, have gone on to become influential classics of political theory.

Claudio Treves and Giuseppe Emanuele Modigliani escaped in 1926, one making his way to Paris via Austria and the other via Switzerland. By late 1926, there was only one major communist or socialist leader who was neither in prison nor in exile. He was the best-known of them all: Filippo Turati.

His lifetime companion, Anna Kuliscioff, died on the 27th of December 1925 after a long illness. Her funeral cortege two days later was attacked by Fascist thugs as it passed through the streets of Milan. Turati, not well himself, was forced to run away from the procession. With both his personal life and all he had fought for collapsing around him, he fell into a major depression. Friends urged him to flee Milan, but he could not rouse himself, despite the fact that Fascists were being heard throughout Milan singing a song whose rhyming refrain was "*Con la barba di Turati noi farem gli spazzolini per lustrar le scarpe di Benito Mussolini*" ("We will use Turati's beard to make the brushes for shining Benito Mussolini's shoes").

At this point Carlo Rosselli, the young editor of *Non Mollare,* entered the picture. Born in 1899 into an elite assimilated Jewish family, Carlo Rosselli was one of three brothers: Sabatino (almost always known as Nello) was a year younger, and Aldo was four years older. They belonged to the fourth generation of a family with a rich tradition of political participation dating back to the *Risorgimento,* Italy's quest for independent unity.

CHAPTER 27

Turati's Escape

GIUSEPPE Emanuele Rosselli, the boys' father, was not interested in a career in politics, nor one in commerce or academia, all traditional careers for young Livorno-born Jews. Politics would have been a natural for this nephew of Rome's mayor Ernesto Nathan and grandson of Sarina Rosselli Nathan, the woman who had befriended and protected Mazzini, but Giuseppe Emanuele, also known simply as Joe, wanted to become a music composer. To perfect his skills he set out, newly married, for Vienna, together his wife, Amelia Pincherle, a young Jewish Venetian hoping to establish herself as a writer. After several years abroad and the birth of their first son they returned to Italy, settling in Rome. His career began spiraling down and hers started to ascend. Unhappy with each other, and by then with three sons, they separated. She moved with her young children to Florence.

Amelia Rosselli, a talented and successful writer of plays, novels, and even children's books, was very well connected and highly regarded in the rich cultural atmosphere of early-twentieth-century Florence. Given their parents' separation and that their father died young in 1911, it is fair to say Giuseppe and Amelia's three sons were raised by their mother. On the other hand, their father's considerable family wealth, willed to them at his death, did play an important role in their life by giving them the means to accomplish many of their aims.

Despite being sympathetic to the Socialist Party's agenda, during World War I Amelia supported the country's entry into the war. Sharing his mother's perspective, her son Aldo volunteered for service even though, as the oldest son of a widowed mother, he could have obtained a deferment. After finding himself assigned to a less active zone, Aldo asked for transfer to the front. He was killed there during the general slaughter the army suffered in 1916. His death and its aftermath were the theme of Amelia Rosselli's 1921 book, *Fratelli Minori* (*Younger Brothers*), a reflection on the agony felt by those left behind.

Carlo and Nello, only a year apart in age, were very different in personality. Nello scholarly, quiet, and reflective, while Carlo was passionate and impulsive. These differences showed up in how they approached their studies and later in their navigation of the changing political waters.

Nello had a traditional education and became a recognized historian. While not an observant Jew, he valued his relation to Judaism, so when he married Maria Tedesco in December of 1926, he and his new bride chose to have a Hebrew service. As he then wrote, "I regard with Jewish severity the duties of our lives on earth, and with Jewish serenity the mystery of life beyond the tomb—because I love all men as in Israel it was commanded."

Carlo, on the other hand, had a checkered early education, wrote a thesis on revolutionary syndicalism, traveled adventurously, ignored his Judaism, and in July of 1926 married Marion Cave, a thirty-year-old Anglican Englishwoman who had come to Florence to participate in what she hoped would be a social revolution. After finishing his degree, Carlo started teaching political economy in Genoa and Milan, so his life involved continual moving between those two cities as well as his home in Florence. This peripatetic existence—and his being a handsome, rich young man—helped him evade suspicion by the Fascists. Carlo's profile did not fit that of a revolutionary intent on overthrowing the regime.

His time in Milan brought him into repeated contact with Turati and a close friendship between the two soon developed with Carlo becoming a frequent visitor to the elder statesman's apartment. As time passed, he became increasingly fearful of what would happen to Turati, should he remain in Milan. Matters took a turn for the worse on October 31, 1926, when a fifteen-year-old boy tried to shoot Mussolini as he drove through Bologna in an open car. The *Duce* was not hurt, but the boy was lynched on the spot, and in the wake of the event, measures that allegedly increased public safety were quickly passed. A new secret police force, the OVRA (*Opera Vigilanza Repressione Anti-Fascismo**), was formed and a Special Tribunal for the Defense of the State was created. Surveillance at the borders also became much stricter.

Alarmed by what was happening, Carlo told Turati that Anna Kuliscioff would not have wanted to see her partner's life end by torture in a Fascist jail. This argument finally convinced Turati to try to escape, and Carlo began formulating a plan. The front door of the building had to be avoided because a Fascist guard was stationed there with the excuse of protecting Turati. In the late afternoon of November 21, Carlo went to Turati's top floor apartment and told him the time had come. Turati shaved off his beard, donned a heavy overcoat, pulled a hat down over his eyes, and, accompanied by Carlo, he gingerly climbed up to the building's shared attic. Making their way to its furthest corner, the two reached an outside ladder that gave access down to an alley. They descended and made their way to a car, waiting for them with its motor running, and managed to leave without being detected by the guard at the front door. It took two days for the Fascists to even realize Turati was no longer in the building. Over the next three weeks a hide-and-seek odyssey took place. Newly tightened Fascist security had made it necessary to abandon the original plans for Turati's escape.

During those weeks, Turati and Carlo moved across Northern Italy from one safe house to another. The usual

* Organization for Vigilance and Repression of Anti-Fascism

border crossings were out of the question and trying to find an unguarded mountain pass over the Alps was ruled out because of Turati's age and poor health. An escape by water from the Italian Riviera coast west of Genoa, neither too far from Milan, nor from the desired safety of France, seemed to offer the best chances. With help from local anti-Fascists, Carlo purchased a boat and hired a small crew. Motoring west along the Riviera coast until reaching French soil seemed likely to lead to capture by patrols, so Carlo decided to try heading directly south toward Corsica.

On the night of December 12, Turati, Carlo, and two fellow anti-Fascists, Sandro Pertini and Ferruccio Parri, boarded the boat.* After a very rough twelve-hour crossing they landed in Calvi, a port on Corsica's northern coast. Local authorities welcomed Turati and his companions, quickly granting political asylum to all of them. Turati and Pertini were soon on their way to mainland France, but Carlo and Parri decided to return to Italy and face the jail terms they were sure to be given. Carlo knew of Mazzini's many tribulations, and he had also heard Anna Kuliscioff, remembering her own sufferings, say that modern youth was afraid of prison. Now, even though his wife Marion was expecting their first child, Carlo felt the time had come for him to take a stand.

Leaving Corsica, he and Parri arrived on the Tuscan coast on December 14th. Immediately arrested, they spent the next ten months being shuttled from one jail to another. Their trial finally began on September 9, 1927, in Savona, the town from which they had left Italy with Turati. Accused of "clandestine expatriation," Carlo and Parri were fortunately tried by the local magistrates rather than the feared Special Tribunal. Carlo let the presiding judge know that he regarded the trial as a political one, adding, "A Rosselli secretly sheltered a dying

*Parri served as Italy's first prime minister after the war, and Pertini later became President of Italy.

Mazzini, an exile in his own country. It was only logical that another Rosselli, a half-century later, tried to save from Fascist fury one of the most noble and unselfish spirits of the country."

The three judges, sympathetic to Carlo and Parri, announced they had concluded that the reason for helping Turati go to France had been his need for specialized medical treatment. The announced punishment was a ten-month sentence, but since that had already been served, the two were free to go. If the judges had said the accuseds' motive was political, the sentence would have been far more severe. Hearing the news, Mussolini telegraphed the Attorney General in nearby Genoa, telling him the two should not go free.

CHAPTER 28

Paris and Turin

CARLO DID NOT go to jail, but he was also not set free. Fascist Italy had developed another way of making sure political undesirables were kept out of circulation: sending them to a *confine*. This was a form of interior exile in which the *confinato* was required to remain within the confines of a small town chosen by the regime. He or she would have to stay there for a fixed amount of time that could vary from months to years. Though under surveillance by the local authorities and not allowed to engage in any political activities, the *confinato* could lead an otherwise normal life. Since the undesirables were usually from industrial Northern Italy where anti-Fascism was more active, the *confino* towns were typically remote ones in Southern Italy.

Carlo Rosselli's term was set at five years and his *confino* was Lipari, a small island off the north coast of Sicily. It was unusual in housing numerous *confinati*, making it similar in some ways to the measures adopted by both the United States and the United Kingdom during World War II to sequester populations whose loyalties they questioned.

Given his financial resources and the freedoms *confinati* were allowed, Carlo was able to rent a small house on the island and have his wife Marion and their newly born son Giovanni join him. He also received visits from his mother and even imported a piano. The authorities reported that he was a model detainee, content with his surroundings.

Unbeknownst to them, Carlo was planning to escape. While waiting to find a way to do so, he was also secretly writing a book summarizing his political views. In June of 1929, in anticipation of an escape attempt, Marion and Giovanni left the island with a draft of the book hidden in their belongings.

Confinati had a curfew of eight o'clock, but on the night of July 26, Carlo and two of his fellow detainees stayed in the surf, waiting to swim out to a motorboat he had arrange to have meet them. It didn't come. They were back in the surf the next night and this time it did. The trio swam out, climbed on board and the boat sped off to nearby Cape Bon in French Tunisia. From there, Carlo made his way to Marseilles and then on to Paris, where he was reunited with Turati, Claudio Treves, Giuseppe Emanuele Modigliani, and many other old friends. The regime's reaction to the escape came swiftly; Marion was sent to prison, but she was a British citizen and an international reaction led by Carlo saw to it that she was quickly released.

Meanwhile, Carlo and associates in Paris were founding a new movement. They named it *Giustizià e Libertà* (Justice and Liberty) and gave it the emblem of a flaming sword against a background of the Italian flag with a G on its left and an L on its right. The leaders insisted on calling it a movement rather than a political party, for they meant it to be a joining of disparate groups with the common aim of overthrowing Italy's Fascist Government and installing a democratic republic. It was a grand, idealistic plan, but *Giustizià e Libertà* was never able to fully settle its rivalries with other anti-Fascist groups active in Paris. Communists took their orders from Moscow and anarchists did not take orders from anyone.

The movement also had difficulties in Italy. *Giustizià e Libertà* quickly began trying to create separate cells in Italy's major cities. Turin, in many ways the most intellectual of Italian cities, as well the major city nearest to Paris, continued to see its cell menaced by several factors, including a rumor being spread that it was controlled by Jews. In addition to Rosselli being Jewish, this rumor was based on an event at the beginning of 1934 when two young Jews from Turin were stopped at the Swiss Italian border town of Ponte Tresa. They were found to be carrying

Giustizià e Libertà printed material. One of them jumped in the nearby river and swam to freedom, but the other was arrested and subsequently so were a dozen or so of his friends, most of them Jews. Fueled by the pro-German wing of the Fascist Party, the right-wing press quickly proclaimed this event to be part of a Jewish plot against the government.

Ettore Ovazza, a prominent Turin Jewish banker and an ardent Fascist, felt the need for a rapid response. In early May he founded a Jewish Fascist newspaper, *La Nostra Bandiera* (Our Flag), telegraphing Mussolini to tell him it portrayed the true Jewish loyalty to the regime. In June, he also helped organize and stack the membership of a new governing board for Turin's Jewish Community to ensure it spoke of the regime in similar terms.

On May 20, Turin's head rabbi, Gino Bolaffio, preached a sermon that went even further. He said,

> We live in the twelfth year of the Fascist era. On Italy's horizon, a bright star has appeared, meant to illuminate the country and the entire civilized world. He is a man of great genius, a spiritual heir of the prophets of Israel....We Jews, educated, as I have said in a school of duty and discipline and not unaware of our Nation's history, remain struck with admiration by the noble figure of *Il Duce*, powerful, gifted with amazing, I would say almost divine, qualities. No, the true Jew does not follow Fascism out of duty, out of opportunism...The true Jew considers Fascism as a providential phenomenon, meant to take him back to God and his forefathers.

It defies credulity that Bolaffio really meant what he was saying, but language in support of dictators often tends to be exaggerated and overly dramatic, especially as Italian easily lends itself to flowery overtones. Since Bolaffio passed away in early 1937, he never had the chance to see how wrong he had been.

The Turin cell of *Giustizià e Libertà* had suffered setbacks in 1934, but worse was yet to come. The following year it faced essential annihilation after being betrayed by an informer who, known in Turin as a Jewish intellectual, had gained the trust of its members and access to their workings. On May 15, 1935, fifty suspected movement members were arrested, and more than two hundred houses were searched for material related to the cell's actions. Those convicted because of the raids were either sent to jail or to *confino.* A high percentage of them were Jews, feeding the growing Fascist suspicion that Jewish intellectuals opposed the regime.

Giustizià e Libertà's success remained limited because, correctly or not, it was viewed as a group of intellectuals and, in some circles, even as a group of Jewish intellectuals. In the fall of 1935, Carlo was further disheartened by the reactions to Italy's bellicose initiatives in Ethiopia. He had hoped these might lead to civil war in Italy but instead the *Duce* was benefiting from his talk of empire.

The cowardice shown by other countries and by the League of Nations in their reluctance to take action against the rise of Fascism in Europe was soon confirmed for Carlo by their responses to the Spanish Civil War. While both Italy and Germany were supplying Franco's armies with airplanes and supplies, Britain and France were refusing to help the forces opposing him. The fight was commonly described as one between nationalists and republicans, but Carlo thought that was a euphemism; for him it was a battle between fascism and socialism. In the late summer of 1936, he set out for the front with other members of *Giustizià e Libertà* and a mix of Italian anarchists, socialists, communists, and republicans; they combined to form an Italian anti-Fascist battalion.

In November of 1936 Carlo beamed a radio broadcast to

Italy from Barcelona, urging fellow Italians to join him in the struggle. Having been wounded in battle and suffering from phlebitis, he then went back to France to recover. In late May of 1937, his brother Nello joined him at Bagnoles-de-l'Orne, a Normandy resort. Having finally been given a passport to leave Italy after years of trying, Nello was looking forward to seeing Carlo; it had been a long separation. On June 9, the brothers took their usual afternoon drive and saw a car by the side of the road with two passengers looking at its open hood. Stopping to see if they could be of assistance, Carlo and Nello were stabbed, their bodies were thrown into the underbrush, and one of the assailants drove their car away. It had been an assassination plot.

Carlo and Nello's bodies were soon recovered and brought to Paris. Their mother only learned of the murder when she arrived in Paris for a planned visit with her sons. People who saw her at the vast funeral that was held said she looked like the figure in a Greek tragedy. But she knew that all her strength was now needed to save her daughters-in-law and their children. She gathered them together and fled to Switzerland; it was the first step in a journey that eventually took them to the United States.

The French authorities discovered a group of seven individuals who had been responsible for planning and carrying out the murder; they were all members of a secret right-wing French Fascist group, closely tied to an Italian counterpart. Though they were placed under arrest, they were all pardoned after the Nazi takeover of France and the installation of Marshal Pétain's puppet government.

CHAPTER 29

The Racial Laws

Mussolini's attitude toward Jews had always been complicated. Though at first he claimed there was no Jewish problem in Italy, it slowly became clear that he harbored suspicion of Jews' allegiance to him. This meant that, unlike in earlier times in Italy, only one Jew, Guido Jung, ever held a cabinet position during the Fascist era. Like many dictators, Mussolini wanted to be sure of his underlings' loyalty.

Despite the occasional talk about a Jewish international financial conspiracy, Mussolini took comparatively little action against Jews until the beginning of the war with Ethiopia in October of 1935. The quick conquest of poorly armed native forces avenged a defeat Italy had incurred there more than a half-century earlier. It gave Mussolini the illusion of possessing a mighty army and allowed Italy to think of itself as a colonial force. The lack of significant opposition by other colonial powers and by the League of Nations—soon reinforced by similar reticence regarding the Spanish Civil War—also led Mussolini to underestimate potential resistance to his actions. With his ego inflated to even higher levels, he began to think he was a military genius and to speak of himself as the *Duce* of a Second Roman Empire.

Meanwhile, Italy was drawing ever closer to its natural ally, Germany. Mussolini increasingly came to admire the man he had once mocked as a pale imitation of himself; one hoping to gain the trappings of authority by calling himself the *Führer* (the German translation of *Duce*). Hitler's ruthlessness and his success in gaining control over all aspects of German life impressed

Mussolini. After the summer of 1936, further impressed by Germany's rearming and by its reoccupation of the Rhineland, Mussolini pushed for the formation of a Rome-Berlin axis. The triumphant reception he received on a state visit to Germany in September of 1937 sealed the bond; a year later, Italy posed no objections to Germany's takeover of Austria, a move it had once strongly resisted.

Mussolini's views on racial differences, already nudged along by his victory in Africa, were magnified by observing the German campaign against Jews. Many Italians thought he was being pressured by Hitler to begin adopting similar measures in Italy, but evidence suggests it was purely Mussolini's decision. On the 14th of July 1938, Mussolini saw to it that a Manifesto of Race was issued. It claimed that Italians were a pure race, and Jews were a non-European one. Contrary to the evidence of the previous hundred years, the document claimed it was impossible to assimilate them into Italian society. Though the Manifesto was signed by many so-called scientific experts on the subject, it appears to have been purely Mussolini's doing. It was soon followed by the publication of a new magazine, *La Difesa della Razza* (*The Defense of the Race*). The cover of the first issue depicts a sword dividing what Mussolini regarded as the classic ideal of beauty from caricatures of an elderly Jewish man and of a young African woman.

Legislative action backing the Manifesto began on September 5, 1938, with a decree stating that Italian citizenship awarded to foreign Jews after January 1, 1919, was revoked with an exception made for those over sixty-five or married to a true Italian. It was the first of a series of such decrees, all designed to deprive Jews of the rights other Italians enjoyed.

On October 6 the Grand Council of Fascism, approved regulations that resembled Germany's infamous 1935 Nuremberg Laws designating who was to be considered as Jewish. Decrees on the 15th of November banned Jews from attending or teaching in public schools, and banned all schools from using texts written by Jewish authors. A November 17th decree dictated that all Jewish members of the armed forces were dismissed, and furthermore that from then on no Jew would be allowed to serve. Limits were also imposed on what Jews could own and who they could employ.

The Italian public did not organize to oppose these measures. The pope, Pius XI, took some small steps by, for instance, appointing the Jewish mathematicians Tullio Levi-Civita and Vito Volterra to the Pontifical Academy of Science, but he did little more. His successor in 1939, Pius XII, was primarily concerned with protecting the status of the Church in what he perceived to be difficult times. The King of Italy, Victor Emanuel III not only approved the new legislation but made sure it was enforced in all aspects of the royal household. As for Mussolini, he now had to find a new dentist.

CHAPTER 30

The Boys of Via Panisperna

THE RACIAL LAWS brought an end to a brief golden age in Italian science. It had lasted scarcely more than a decade, but it was significant for the whole world, not just for Italy.

Until the early 1920s, Italian universities considered physics a minor, purely experimental subject, unimportant enough that it could be handled by a single university professor with the aid of an assistant. Topics such as mechanics and wave theory, now included in physics department curriculums, were taught in the much larger and more prestigious mathematics departments. New areas of physics like radioactivity and atomic structure were emerging, and the novel specialty of theoretical physics was being created. Men like Max Planck, Albert Einstein, and Niels Bohr, all Northern Europeans, were leading the studies of relativity and quantum theory.

It was unclear how Italian universities might proceed, but then, in the early 1920s, came an extraordinary piece of good fortune for Italy and its universities: the arrival on the scene of Enrico Fermi. Born in Rome in 1901 to modest parents who were educated but had never attended university, he decided at a young age to be a physicist, even though he was not quite sure what that meant. Essentially self-taught, he went on to become Italy's greatest scientist since Galileo.

Thankfully, Orso Corbino, a far-seeing Rome senior physics professor, quickly recognized Fermi's talent. With the support of Rome's mathematicians, he persuaded the university to create a chair of theoretical physics, and they made sure that Fermi would be chosen to fill the position. At twenty-six, he was now not only a professor at Italy's major university but the country's youngest professor.

Welcomed into the society of Rome's Jewish mathematicians, Fermi was soon also attending the Saturday evening gatherings at the Castelnuovos' house. Straddling physics and mathematics, he comfortably moved from one of their two living rooms to the other, discussing university matters with the mathematicians in the first one and leaving after a while to join their children in the second one. He was, after all, much closer in age to them than to their parents.

Since Fermi loved hiking in the mountains and enjoyed the company of the Castelnuovo circle, it was quite natural for him to also spend part of his summer vacation with them at their village retreat in the Dolomites, a chain of mountains in northwest Italy. That is where he met their daughter Gina's best friend. Laura was the daughter of Admiral Augusto Capon—like Castelnuovo, a Venetian Jew. A summer romance between Laura and the new physics professor turned into something more serious. Laura and Enrico married in 1928.

My uncle Emilio first met Fermi in 1927, thanks to his best friend at the time, mathematician Federigo Enriques' son, Giovanni, a fellow undergraduate engineering student. He told Emilio that his father said a new genius was joining the physics department and he was likely to be looking for students. This sounded interesting, and Emilio quickly becamc Fermi's first student. It was the beginning of a tight working relation that lasted until Emilio was awarded his own professorship a decade later.

A group of five young men soon formed a working team with Fermi, who—almost uniquely in twentieth-century physics—was both a great theoretical physicist and an experimental one. Their team came to be known in the popular press as the Boys of Via Panisperna, an old Roman street that housed the university's physics department. Since the university had no central campus, departments were scattered throughout the city, and physics was housed in an old *palazzo* at that address. Under Fermi's leadership the core group went on to do world-famous nuclear physics experiments during the 1930s. They also had fun together, going hiking, skiing, and playing practical jokes on outsiders as well as on one another. Each went by a nickname: Fermi, regarded as infallible, was the Pope, while his old college friend Franco Rasetti was the Cardinal, and Emilio, known for his difficult personality, was the *Basilisco,* a fire-spitting monster of legend. This was all very different from the prevailing staid atmosphere in academic departments.

The fame of the Via Panisperna boys spread rapidly, and young would-be physicists began coming to Rome to study with them. Not all those who came were even physicists. For instance, Salvatore Luria, the Italian Jewish Nobel Prize–winning molecular biologist claims that the year he spent with the physicists after getting his medical degree in Turin was crucial for his career.

Several up-and-coming theoretical physicists from Northern Europe also began coming to Rome to work with and learn from Fermi; he was much less formal than the German professors they had studied with, and his approach was unlike what they had learned was the correct way to approach a problem. As one of them, Rudolf—later Sir Rudolf—Peierls wrote of him, "His methods were always simple, and he did not like complicated techniques. When a problem became complicated, he lost interest. But it must be explained that in Fermi's hands, problems that had been terrifyingly complicated for others often became very simple."

This group from the North, which included several future Nobel Prize winners, certainly profited from and enjoyed their stay in Rome. But the stream died out after 1933 because most of those individuals had been Jews, and they now had other things on their minds, chiefly how to escape the onslaught of Nazism. They were busy looking for positions in the United States or Great Britain.

Fermi tried to ignore politics, concentrating completely on work and family, but the Italian group around him was disappearing. His old friend and co-worker Franco Rasetti, disgusted by the advance of Fascism in Italy, left for Canada, and my uncle Emilio went to the United States. Bruno Pontecorvo, a Jew from Pisa who was the youngest and probably the most promising of the young Via Panisperna boys, fled as well, going first to Paris and then across the Atlantic. By mid-1938, only Fermi and Edoardo Amaldi were left in the group.

Fermi could no longer blot out what was happening around him. He had thought of leaving Italy but had not made plans to do so because Laura loved Rome and did not want to leave her old father, now a widower. But when Racial Laws began passing in 1938, Enrico said this was too much. She and their two children might be in danger. After hearing he was going to be awarded the Physics Nobel Prize that fall, he began hatching a plan. The Fermi family would go to Stockholm in December for the ceremony and then, with money from the prize in hand, they would board an ocean liner bound for New York. New York was their new home, and after the war they moved to Chicago. The Fermis would never again live in Italy.

Italy's brief golden age of physics had come to an end. The United States was fortunate to have welcomed Fermi, for he would play a key role in the development of nuclear energy, the making of the first atomic bomb, and in the progress of physics in the post-war United States.

Fermi made his first trip back to Italy in the fall of 1949, delivering six lectures on contemporary problems in physics. He was introduced at the first one, a ceremonial occasion, by Guido Castelnuovo, the dean of Italy's university professors and now also the president of the reconstituted *Accademia dei Lincei.* A quarter-century earlier, Castelnuovo had enthusiastically supported young Fermi's appointment to the Rome faculty, had welcomed him into his social circle, and his own daughter had introduced him to Laura. Now he was welcoming back, after an eleven-year absence, one of the true greats of modern science, emphasizing in his opening remarks that he hoped the return would be an inspiration for a new generation of Italian physicists—and it was.

Finale

THIS BOOK has attempted to describe the lives of Italian Jews during an almost one-hundred-year period, bookmarked by their integration into Italian society at one end and their abandonment by the Italian Government at the other end. There is no doubt that during these years Italian Jews—in their heyday, a small group of forty-five thousand or so out of a total Italian population of forty-five million—made major contributions to their country's rapid evolution from a culturally rich but impoverished agrarian country to an economically developed one.

If one wants to pick a simplistic version of the Golden Age's beginning and end, it is tempting to say it started on the morning of September 20, 1870, when a Piedmontese Jew, Captain Giacomo Segre, *received* the order to breach the walls of Rome, and it ended on October 28, 1922, when another Piedmontese Jew, General Emanuele Pugliese, *did not receive* the order to defend the walls of Rome against the Fascists.

The difficulty in selecting a particular date, at least for the beginning of this golden age, is underscored by Italy not yet existing as a nation in 1848. Looking at Rome, one is tempted to pick a later year, while in Florence the starting date would be earlier. As for the Italian South, the *Mezzogiorno,* the question is almost irrelevant, for the region harbored scarcely any Jews, and did not benefit from economic development comparable to what took place in Italy's northern half.

Despite these observations, the most obvious designation for the beginning of the golden age is the Kingdom of Sardinia's issuance of its *Statuto Albertino* in 1848, since it codified Jews' equality before the law. Later, it became the nation's constitution when the Kingdom of Italy was proclaimed in 1861. It also remained in place, though modified under Fascism, until the official end of the monarchy in 1948.

Selecting a date for the end of the golden age poses other challenges. It is tempting to place it at the 1922 March on Rome, the action that led to the Fascist takeover. But many Jews thought otherwise at the time. Often blinded by their fear of a revolutionary leftist takeover, they dismissed their increasing exclusion from positions of power. They were wrong. Even if neither the March on Rome, nor Matteotti's 1924 assassination, nor the 1936 Ethiopian War is chosen as terminus, the golden age was waning after 1922. But its unmistakably final moment was the 1938 passage of the Racial Laws depriving Italian Jews of the rights enjoyed by other Italian citizens.

Thinking that life would continue to remain at least tolerable, almost none foresaw that five years later they would experience the greatest tragedy of their two-thousand-year history on Italian soil. The suffering it entailed has been described by many distinguished historians and by several great authors, including Jewish ones such as Alberto Moravia, Natalia Ginzburg, and the incomparable Primo Levi. Its memory remains a scar in Italian history.

The Italian Jews who fled have enriched the culture of their new countries. The number remaining in Italy has diminished from forty-five to thirty thousand out of a total population that has grown from forty-five to sixty million. Half of Italy's remaining Jews live in Rome and two thirds of the others reside in Milan. Though well respected, they no longer play the exceptional role they once did. Italian Jews' golden age, already waning for twenty years, truly ended in 1938.

Acknowledgments

I would like to thank my family and my many friends who good-naturedly listened to me telling some of the stories in this book. You know who you are. My stepson Jason Yaffe and his wife Suzanne read parts of an earlier version of the manuscript and offered helpful remarks, as did my brother Giuseppe (Joseph) and his wife Jessica. Finally, I am indebted as ever to my wife, Bettina Hoerlin, for her loving support, for her continued incisive criticism, and, last but perhaps not least, for patiently putting up with me as I carried on at length about some obscure bit of Italian history.

I would very much like to thank my publisher Paul Dry Books for their stalwart encouragement to write this combination of history and family memoir. I am grateful to Julia Sippel for a very fine and careful job of editing that has greatly improved the book. Mara Brandsdorfer and Maude de Moll Kushto at Paul Dry Books have also contributed significantly to bringing the book to completion.

References

NOTE

This book is not a memoir, for although my parents, grandparents, and other relatives appear in it, I essentially do not. Having lived most of my life in the United States but with a substantial part of my formative years and schooling in Italy, it is rather my personal attempt to understand my roots; a journey that led me to examine the broader picture of how Italian Jews managed to integrate into Italian society, achieve so much, and contribute so greatly to a new and developing Italy.

The references are largely those that have aided me in this quest and therefore may occasionally lack the balance a trained historian would aim to provide. When possible, they are presented in either English or English translations. The chosen format is slightly unusual, but one I have used before, as in my book *A Matter of Degrees*, published in 2002 by Viking Press. I believe this format is particularly well-suited to this book. There is a reference section for each chapter of the book that provides a list of the sources of the quotes and the references that have been used in the writing of that chapter, as well as some additional ones, should the reader wish to pursue matters further, and any occasional comments by the author.

GENERAL REFERENCES

For a short, incisive view of Italian Jewish history, there is no better reference than the historian Arnaldo Momigliano's four-page essay *The Jews of Italy* that appeared on pages 22-26 of the 10/24/1985 issue of the *New York Review of Books.*

For a general history of Italian Jews, the most comprehensive reference, unfortunately not available in an English translation, is Attilio Milano's 1963 *Storia degli Ebrei in Italia,* Einaudi, Turin. I will refer to it as Attilio Milano 1963 in what follows.

Cecil Roth's 1946 *The History of the Jews of Italy,* Jewish Publication Society of America, Philadelphia, is an older standard reference.

Good sources in English of more recent Italian Jewish history that I have found especially useful are:

Shira Klein. 2018. *Italy's Jews from Emancipation to Fascism.* Cambridge University Press, New York.

Michele Sarfatti. 2006. *The Jews in Mussolini's Italy: From Equality to Persecution.* Translated by John and Anne C. Tedeschi. University of Wisconsin Press, Madison.

Elizabeth Schächter. 2011. *The Jews of Italy, 1848-1915: Between Tradition and Transformation.* Vallentine Mitchell, London

One invaluable source that deserves special mention is the *Dizionario Biografico degli Italiani,* which we will refer to as Diz. Bi.It. in what follows. Published by Rome's *Istituto dell'Enciclopedia Italiana,* it is a hundred volumes of biographies of over forty thousand distinguished Italians. The entries, written over the course of many years by experts in their respective fields and signed by the authors, are relatively short (typically about five thousand words) but complete biographies, with numerous references to correspondence and even unpublished manuscripts. Available online, they are particularly useful in the case of individuals from the past who are distinguished but perhaps not enough so to warrant a full-scale modern biography.

Prologue

The quote *"Faith, for the old ones...."* is from a privately published memoir written for her family in 1990 by Silvia Treves Levi Vidale, my father's first cousin. It is entitled *All'Ombra Degli Avi* (*In the Shadow of Ancestors*).

1: October 1943

An excellent reference is Susan Zuccotti's 1987 *The Italians and the Holocaust: Persecution, Rescue, and Survival*, Basic Books, New York.

Alexander Stille's 1991 *Benevolence and Betrayal: Five Italian Jewish Families Under Fascism*, Summit Books, New York documents vividly the lives of five families during this period and contains an extensive set of references for further reading. It is an excellent and very readable resource.

Chapter XII of Riccardo Calimani's 2013 *Storia degli Ebrei Italiani: Nel XIX e nel XX secolo*, Mondadori, Milan is also very helpful regarding the events of this period.

Liliana Picciotto Fargion's 1991 *Il Libro della Memoria: Gli Ebrei Deportati dall'Italia (1943-1945)*, Mursia, Milan contains brief biographical sketches of the deported. See also the essay "*Testimonianza di un deportato da Roma*," in Liliana Picciotto Fargion's 1979 *L'occupazione tedesca e gli ebrei di Roma: Documenti e fatti*, Carucci, Rome

Her editing of documents includes the quote, *"You are going toward your death...."* given to her by Arminio Wachsberger.

The quote *"You are right in going...."* is from page 130 of my uncle Emilio's autobiography,

Emilio Segrè. 1999. *A Mind Always in Motion.* University of California Press, Berkeley.

The quote *"The tragic and painful page...."* is from page 195 of the same book.

The historian Michele Sarfatti is the director of the *Centro di Documentazione Ebraica Contemporanea* in Milan and Italy's foremost expert on the conditions of Italian Jews during Fascism. He is also a member of numerous government committees charged with documenting their sufferings during thar era. His only book in an English edition is his 2006 *The Jews in Mussolini's Italy: From Equality to Persecution,* translated by John and Anne C. Tedeschi, University of Wisconsin Press, Madison. Other important works by him are his 2005 *La Shoah in Italia: la persecuzione degli ebrei sotto il fascismo,* Einaudi, Turin, and his 2018 *Gli ebrei nell'Italia fascista: Vicende, identità, persecuzione,* Einaudi, Turin.

Together with Anna Sarfatti, he has also co-authored children's books about Jews during the Fascist era.

2: All Families are not alike

The quote, *"Chi fuor li maggiori tui"* is from Canto X of Dante Alighieri's *La Divina Commedia,* edited by C. H. Grandgent, D.C. Heath &Co., Boston—bilingual edition from 1933.

The story of J. Robert Oppenheimer informing my uncle Emilio that his mother had been seized by the Nazis is told on p. 195 of Emilio Segrè's autobiography, *A Mind Always in Motion.*

The University of Florence's Prof. Patrizia Guarnieri has prepared an online volume *Intellectuals Displaced from Fascist Italy.* It includes a description of my father's life and career, which can be found by looking up "Angelo Segrè" on Guarnieri's site, www.intellettualinfuga.com.

Information is also available in Mattia Balbo's biography of him in the Diz.Bi.It.

3: 2000 Years of Jewish Rome

My knowledge of Italian Jewish history before 1700 has greatly benefited from reading Attilio Milano 1963 and his 1988 *Il Ghetto di Roma*, Carucci, Rome. The stories about how Italian Jews had to humiliatingly swear their loyalty to Rome and their maltreatment during Carnevale are drawn from the latter's Chapter Eleven.

Riccardo Calimani's 2016 *Storia degli Ebrei Italiani: Dalle Origini al XV Secolo*, Mondadori, Milan. is another valuable resource for Italian Judaism before the fifteenth century.

The story of Jews walking through the Arch of Titus on December 2, 1947, is told on pp. 386-387 of Augusto Segre's 1979 *Memorie di Vita Ebraica: Casale Monferrato, Roma Gerusalemme, 1918-1960*, Bonacci, Rome.

Pope Paul IV's papal bull *Cum Nimis Absurdum* is available online. A commentary on its contents' effect on Roman Jews can be found at:

David Berger. 1979. "*Cum Nimis Absurdum* and the Conversion of the Jews." Jewish Quarterly Review. New Series. 70 (1): 41–49.

History lovers can find this book by the great nineteenth-century German historian Ferdinand Gregorovius in its 1948 re-published form, *The Ghetto and the Jews of Rome*, translated by Moses Hadas, Schocken Books, New York.

There is also, of course, the eternal classic, Suetonius, *The Twelve Caesars*, Penguin Classics, London.

4: The Comings and Goings of Italian Jews

I consulted Attilio Milano 1963 pp.167-178 for details of the presence of Jews in Southern Italy (particularly Sicily) before their expulsion in 1492. This expulsion occurred because the island and a large part of the region had come under Spanish rule.

The history of the Venice ghetto can be found in Riccardo Calimani's 1987, *The Ghetto of Venice,* translated by Katherine Silberblatt Wolfthal, M. Evans & Co., New York.

Alessandro Manzoni's 1827 *The Betrothed,* available in a 2022 translation by Michael F. Moore, Modern Library Classics, New York, is considered Italy's most important historical novel.

The story of my father's cousin Renzo Ravenna's time as *podestà* (Fascist mayor) of Ferrara is told in Ilaria Pavan's 2006 *Il podesta` ebreo: La storia di Renzo Ravenna tra fascismo e leggi razziali,* Laterza, Bari.

Giorgio Bassani's 1977 *The Garden of the Finzi-Continis,* Harcourt, Brace and Jovanovich, Boston, has become a very well-known book. It was also made into a successful movie, directed by the legendary Vittorio de Sica.

H. Stuart Hughes' 1983 *Prisoners of Hope: The Silver Age of the Italian Jews 1924-1974,* Harvard University Press, Cambridge, Mass., analyzes *The Garden of the Finzi-Continis* and other writings by Bassani in conjunction with an illuminating discussion of writings by other major Italian Jewish post-WWII writers, namely Natalia Ginzburg, Alberto Moravia, and Primo Levi.

5: The Winds of Tolerance and Freedom

The issuing by Emperor Joseph of the 1782 Edict of Tolerance, the subsequent actions in France, and the effect of Napoleon's descent into Italy is well described on p. 21-22 of Shira Klein's 2018 *Italy's Jews from Emancipation to Fascism*, Cambridge University Press, New York.

The Edgardo Mortara story is beautifully told in David Kertzer's 1997 *The Kidnapping of Edgardo Mortara*, Vintage Books, New York.

There were numerous documented cases of Jewish children being forcibly baptized in early-nineteenth-century Italy. Riccardo Calimani's 2013 *Storia degli Ebrei Italiani: Nel XIX e nel XX secolo*, Mondadori, Milan provides examples on pages 76-80.

Calimani's book also describes Pius IX's initial benevolence toward Jews on pages 31-32.

The full text of *Quanta Cura* is available online. The reaction to it is described on p. 85 of Denis Mack Smith's 1969 *Modern Italy: A Political History*, University of Michigan Press, Ann Arbor, and on pp. 23-24 of David Kertzer's 2004 *Prisoner of the Vatican*, Houghton Mifflin, Boston.

6: The Golden Age Commences

For both a guide to Italian synagogues, Jewish cemeteries, and their history see:

Annie Sacerdoti and Luca Fiorentino. 1989. *Guide to Jewish Italy*. Israelowitz, Brooklyn.

For a general history in English of the Italian nineteenth-century drive to unification, commonly known as the *Risorgimento*, see:

Derek Beales and Eugenio Biagini. 2003. *The Risorgimento and the Unification of Italy.* Routledge, London.

Lucy Riall. 1994. *The Italian Risorgimento: State, Society and National Unification.* Routledge, London.

Lucy Riall. 2009. *Risorgimento: The History of Italy from Napoleon to Nation State.* Palgrave Macmillan, London.

Denis Mack Smith, the late British author, was very prolific in his writings about the history of Italy in the years from the *Risorgimento* up to modern times. His work includes biographies of the four main figures in Italy's drive to unification: Cavour, Garibaldi, Mazzini, and Victor Emanuel II. His 1997 *Modern Italy: A Political History*, University of Michigan Press, Ann Arbor has been a very useful source of information for me.

7: The Final Battle for the Papal State

For an account of September 20, 1870, in Rome, see Hubert Heyries' 2020 *La Breccia di Porta Pia: 20 Settembre 1870*, Il Mulino Bologna.

Giacomo Segre's story is told in Vero Fazio's 2021, *Il Seguito della Storia: Giacomo e Roberto Segre tra Breccia di Porta Pia e Grande Guerra*, Belforte, Livorno. It includes an account of how Giacomo Segre's son Roberto became a general in the Italian Army during WWI.

The episode of Riccardo Mortara's 1870 encounter with his brother Edgardo is told on p. 263 of David Kertzer's, 1998 *The Kidnapping of Edgardo Mortara*, Vintage Books, New York.

The battle for Rome is also described in David Kertzer's 2004 *Prisoner of the Vatican*, Houghton Mifflin, Boston.

Alfonso La Marmora, a former commander in the Italian Army and a former prime minister of Italy from 1864 to 1866, was considered an ideal choice for the 1870 negotiations with the Papal State. Appointed as lieutenant general in charge of the Roman provinces, it would be his last assignment. For those interested in a biography of his life, see Giuseppe Massari's 1880 *Il Generale Alfonso La Marmora,* Barbèra, Florence.

8: Two Deaths: the King and the Pope

The stories of the deaths of Victor Emanuel II and Pope Pius IX are told very well in Chapter 10, "Two Deaths," of David Kertzer's 2004 *Prisoner of the Vatican,* Houghton Mifflin, Boston.

Pages 292-293 of this book also describe the negotiation of the 1929 Lateran Treaty between Mussolini's government and the Papacy. This treaty and the Concordat that followed led, almost sixty years after the 1870 battle for Rome, to the Vatican formally recognizing the Kingdom of Italy and Rome as its capital. The Vatican agreeing to the treaty implicitly gave legitimacy to the Fascist regime. In return, the Kingdom of Italy recognized the Vatican City and made concessions to it, including financial ones, and acknowledged Catholicism as Italy's official religion. The treaty also made Catholic instruction obligatory in public schools. In addition, Italy from then on ceased recognizing the 20th of September as a national holiday.

Frank J. Coppa's October 2003 "Pio Nono and the Jews: from 'Reform' to 'Reaction,' 1846 to 1878," *The Catholic Historical Review,* Vol. 89, No. 4, Catholic University of America Press, Washington D.C., may also be of interest.

9: Rome's Jewish Mayor

The entire text of *Etsi Multa Luctosa* can be found online in English at www.papalencyclicals.net.

Michele Sarfatti has written an interesting article titled "*Vittorio Emanuele III nel settembre 1910 voleva sostituire Luigi Luzzatti perché ebreo?*" that deals with Nathan's September 20th, 1910, speech and the reaction to it by the Catholic Church. It includes a reference to Nathan's full speech on that occasion. See: https://www.michelesarfatti.it/documenti-e-commenti/vittorio-emanuele-iii-nel-settembre-1910-voleva-sostituire-luigi-luzzatti-perche-ebreo.

Italy's interest in Nathan's mayoralty remains high as one can see from the continued publication of books on his life and term as mayor. This is a list of four of them:

Nadia Ciani. 2007. *Da Mazzini al Campidoglio: Vita di Ernesto Nathan.* Ediesse, Rome.

Maria Immacolata Macioti. 2021. *Nathan: Il sindaco di Roma dalla parte del popolo.* Iaccobelli, Rome.

Fabio Martini. 2007. *Nathan e l'invenzione di Roma: Il sindaco che cambiò la Città eterna.* Marsilio, Venice

Romano Ugolini. 2003. *Ernesto Nathan tra idealità e pragmatismo.* Edizioni dell'Ateneo, Rome.

10: The Mayor's Mother

The rise of Livorno as a commercial center offering favorable conditions to Jews is well treated on pp. 322-328 Attilio Milano 1963. The section is appropriately entitled, "*L'Oasi di Livorno*" ("The Livorno Oasis"), a reference to Livorno being a safe haven for Jews, particularly ones fleeing Spain and Portugal.

Giuseppe Monsagrati, a history professor at Rome's La Sapienza University, has written an excellent biography of Sarina Levi Nathan in Diz.Bi.It.

For more information on Mazzini, see Denis Mack Smith's 1994 *Mazzini,* Yale University Press, New Haven, or Mazzini's own crucial outline of his beliefs in Giuseppe Mazzini's 1862 *The Duties of Man*, Chapman & Hall, London.

11: Two Tuscan Barons Study the Mafia

Leopoldo's family background, similar in many ways to Sonnino's, is discussed on pp. 286-288 of Riccardo Calimani's 2013 *Storia degli Ebrei Italiani: Nel XIX e nel XX secolo*, Mondadori, Milan.

A quote in Arnaldo Momigliano's October 24, 1985 *New York Review of Books* article "The Jews of Italy" is telling regarding Sonnino and Franchetti's interest in agriculture. He writes on p.23 that the most important new opportunity for Italian Jews in the second half of the nineteenth century was

> ...the possibility of becoming farmers and landowners. Italian Jews, especially of Piedmont, Veneto, Emilia and Tuscany, were indeed strongly inclined to buy land and settle on or near it.

Emilio Sereni's 1997 *History of the Italian Agricultural Scene*, Princeton University Press, Princeton, originally published in Italian in 1961, is a classic work describing the history of Italian agriculture from antiquity to the mid-twentieth century in a social, economic, and ecological context. Sereni was a prominent Jewish Italian anti-Fascist resistance fighter in WWII and a Communist politician.

Sonnino remains a somewhat enigmatic figure on the Italian scene, extraordinarily gifted intellectually, but often rigid and intransigent. He was occasionally described as being more like an English country gentleman than an Italian politician. Though some labeled him a Jew, Judaism seems to have had very little influence on his life. A life-long bachelor, he remained very close to his mother, an Anglican, and distant from his father. A great deal of what I learned about him about him comes from the excellent collection of essays edited by Pier Luigi Ballini: 2000. *Sidney Sonnino e il suo Tempo.* Leo Olschki, Florence.

"The honorable Sonnino, dedicating himself early in his life to politics...." is a quote from Giovanni Giolitti's 1982 *Memorie della mia Vita,* Garzanti, Milan. It is also quoted on p. VI of Ballini's book.

I opened with some trepidation the book Sonnino and Franchetti wrote about their Sicilian trip:

Sidney Sonnino and Leopoldo Franchetti. 1925. *La Sicilia nel 1876.* Vallecchi, Florence.

I am pleased to report it is readable, well written, and interesting, particularly in its analysis of Sicilian banditry.

For more information about Alice Hallgarten Franchetti, see Maria Luciana Buseghin's chapter "Alice Hallgarten Franchetti: A Woman Beyond Barriers," in the 2022 book *A Female Activist Elite in Italy (1890–1920),* edited by Elena Laurenzi and Manuela Mosca, Springer Professional, New York.

12: Opportunity

To appraise what opportunities Italian Jews had, learning about the literacy and health, etcetera of Italians during the nineteenth century is a necessity. Fortunately, statistics about these and many other aspects of life have been compiled by Italy's National Statistics Bureau, ISTAT—Istituto Nazionale di Statistica, Via Cesare Balbo 16, Rome: https://www.istat.it.

The conditions in agriculture at that time are discussed in Emilio Sereni's 1997 *History of the Italian Agricultural Scene*, Princeton University Press, Princeton.

The conditions in the schools are examined in Giovanni Genovesi's 2010 *Storia della scuola in Italia dal Settecento a oggi*, Laterza, Bari.

Jews seem to have had literacy rates that were twice as high as that of the population at large (see Shira Klein's *Italy's Jews from Emancipation to Fascism*, p. 31, for references).

For the education of Jews see Chapter VIII of Attilio Milano 1963. This chapter also has an interesting discussion of Jews' training in medicine over the centuries.

13: Acceptance

Looking back at the record, the acceptance and influence of Jews seems to have peaked in the first two decades of the twentieth century. Though only a tenth of one percent of the Italian population, they had reached the highest positions in government and the military, constituted almost ten percent of university faculty, and two dozen Jews sat in the royally nominated senate. For details about these statistics see pp. 188-189, 217-219, and 230 of Guido Bedarida's 1950 *Ebrei d'Italia*, Tirrena, Livorno.

Shira Klein's *Italy's Jews from Emancipation to Fascism* has a particularly good section on pages 30-39 about the rise and acceptance of Italian Jewry.

The Maurogonato case is discussed in e.g. p.37 of Maurizio Molinari's 1991 *Ebrei in Italia: un problema di identità (1870-1938)*, Giuntina, Florence.

14: Assimilation

This chapter is a profile of a Jew who reached the highest ranks of government while fully assimilating and yet still maintained a strong Jewish identity. Luigi Luzzatti, born in Venice in 1841, was an author, a university professor, a member of Parliament for fifty years, a Minister of the Treasury, and at one point even Italy's Prime Minister.

The details of Luigi Luzzatti's childhood, education, and subsequent attitudes toward Judaism are described in Chapter 3, "*Luigi Luzzatti e l'Ebraismo*," pp. 59-79 of Mario Toscano's 2019 *Ebrei e Ebraismo nell'Italia del Novecento*, Franco Angeli, Rome.

Luzzatti's beliefs are also discussed on pp. 269-274 of Riccardo Calimani's *Storia degli Ebrei Italiani: Nel XIX e nel XX secolo.*

Luzzatti's writings on religion are available in English in a 2005 edition of Luigi Luzzatti's *God in Freedom: Studies in the Relations Between Church and State*, translated by Alfonso Arbib-Costa, Cosimo Classics, New York.

His memoirs are published as:

Luigi Luzzatti. 1935. *Memorie Tratte dal Carteggio.* Zanichelli, Bologna

The quote *"I know only one homeland……"* is from p. 76 of the above and is also given on p. 61 of Toscano's book.

15: The Moncalvos

The details of Enrico Castelnuovo' childhood, education, and subsequent career are drawn from Benito Recchilongo's biography of him in Diz.Bi.It.

The Enrico Castelnuovo novel discussed in this section is also available in English as Enrico Castelnuovo's 2017 *The Moncalvos*, translated by Brenda Webster and Gabriella Romani, Wings Press, San Antonio. The following quotes are all from this book.

"there are too many of these barons. . . ." p.82
"Her American friends will be competing. . . ." p.29
"joy in Heaven to see the return of one" p.183
"The Jewess, the Jewess. . . ." 197
"Our grandparents were orthodox. . . ." p.15

16: Castelnuovo's Son

The lives and careers of the great mathematicians Guido Castelnuovo, Federigo Enriques, Tullio Levi-Civita, Francesco Sever, and Vito Volterra are intertwined. Their stories are very well told in the following publications by the distinguished American historian of science Judith Goodstein:

Judith Goodstein. 2007. *The Volterra Chronicles: The life and Times of an Extraordinary Mathematician: 1860-1940*. American Mathematical Society, Providence.

Judith Goodstein. 2010. *Einstein's Italian Mathematicians: Ricci, Levi-Civita, and the Birth of General Relativity*. American Mathematical Society, Providence.

The quote *"There are two good things about Italy: spaghetti and Levi-Civita"* appears on p. 131 of Donald Babbitt and Judith Goodstein's "Federigo Enriques' Attempt to Prove the 'Completeness Theorem,'" *Notices of the American Mathematical Society*, 58 (2011): 240-249.

"Space-time tells matter how to move; matter tells space-time how to curve" is a quote from John Archibald Wheeler's and Kenneth Ford's 2000 *Geons, Black Holes and Quantum Foam: A Life in Physics*. W.W. Norton &Co., New York

17: Lombardy Great Grandparents

My cousin Claudio Segrè, a financier, has taken a special interest in the history of Judaism and Jews in Bozzolo. He has also provided funds for the restoration of the city's Jewish Cemetery and has co-authored a book about the city's Jewish history:

Claudio Segrè and Ludovico Bettoni. 2000. *Dall'Ancien Regime all' Età Borghese: Bozzolo, la Comunità Ebraica e le sue famiglie (1597-1955)*. Grafo, Brescia.

Ermanno Finzi's 2017 *E alla Fine Non Rimase Nessuno,* Istituto Mantovano di Storia Contemporanea, Mantua also tells the story of Jews in Bozzolo and three other small nearby communities.

18: Their Three Boys

Information about the Collegio Ghislieri and its history is available on their website.

Biographies of the brothers Claudio and Gino Segrè can be found in Diz.Bi.It.

If interested in the history of Italian railroads, you can consult Italo Briano's 1977 *Storia delle ferrovie in Italia,* Cavallotti Editore, Milan.

Primo Levi's 1961 *Survival in Auschwitz,* translated by Stuart Woolf, Collier Books, New York, was first published in Italy in 1947, but there was little interest in Holocaust studies at the time, and it was largely ignored. It did not become a major success until it was reissued by the Turin publishing house of Einaudi in 1958.

19: Tuscan Great Grandparents

Accounts of early Jewish life in Florence can be found in Attilio Milano 1963 on pp. 123-124, 199-201, 262-264, 327-328 and in Roberto G. Salvadori's 2000 *Gli Ebrei di Firenze, Giuntina, Florence.*

The information in this section about Marco Treves' life, marriage, and career is from my father's cousin's privately published monograph, Silvia Treves Levi Vidale's 1990 *All'Ombra Degli Avi* (*In the Shade of the Ancestors*).

20: The Florence Synagogue

Some further details about the synagogue are available on pages 158-161 of Annie Sacerdoti and Luca Fiorentino's 1989 *Guide to Jewish Italy*, Israelowitz, Brooklyn.

Almost all the information in this section is once again gleaned from Silvia Treves Levi Vidale's 1990 *All'Ombra Degli Avi* (*In the Shade of the Ancestors*).

The quote *"I can say that in this very religious atmosphere...."* is also from this book.

Samuel Margulies' life and contributions as Florence's Chief Rabbi are discussed on pages 207-209 of Elizabeth Schächter's 2011 *The Jews of Italy, 1848-1915: Between Tradition and Transformation*, Vallentine Mitchell, London.

21: Italian Zionism: Jewish or Italian?

Zionism is discussed at length in Chapter 5 of Elizabeth Schächter's 2011 *The Jews of Italy, 1848-1915: Between Tradition and Transformation*, Vallentine Mitchell, London. Starting with discussing Zionism's roots in Western Europe, this book goes on, from page 165 to page 205, to detail the forms Zionism took in Italy. It presents at length three branches of Italian Zionism (*sionismo in Italian*), one led by the Federazione Sionistica Italiana, a second by Rabbi Samuel Margulies and his Rabbinical College, and a third articulated by Dante Lattes in his role as editor of the Triestine *Corriere Israelitico.*

The quote *"Egli appartiene ai più fanatici...."* is from p.175 of Schächter's book.

Two books about Italian Zionism that may be of interest are:

Francesco Del Canuto. 1972. *Il Movimento sionistico in Italia dalle origini al 1924.* Federazione Sionistica Italiana, Milano.

Dante Lattes.1928. *Il Sionismo.* Cremonese, Rome.

22: The Grand Lady of Italian Socialism

Diz.Bi.It. contains an informative biography of Anna Kuliscioff written by Mariapia Bigaran, as well as an equally informative one of Filippo Turati written by Giovanni Scirocco.

Two full biographies of Anna Kuliscioff have also appeared in Italian. They are Maria Casalini's1987 *La signora del socialismo italiano: Vita di Anna Kuliscioff,* Editori Riuniti, Rome and Franco Damiani and Fabio Rodriguez's 1978 *Anna Kuliscioff: Immagini, scritti, testimonianze,* Feltrinelli Economica, Milan.

Kuliscioff's influential 1890 Feminist tract has recently been republished in an English translation as:

Anna Kuliscioff. 2021. *The Monopoly of Man.* Translated by Lorenzo Chiesa. MIT Press, Cambridge.

Spencer Di Scala's 1980 *Dilemmas of Italian Socialism: The Politics of Filippo Turati,* University of Massachusetts Press, Amherst helps the reader understand Turati's actions and thoughts.

23: Dueling Socialists: Treves and Mussolini

References to Mussolini's life and career are listed in the section for Chapter 26.

24 Emilia is an online Italian journal (www.24emilia.com) based in Reggio Emilia. It provides news of the region, international news, and occasional in-depth essays about historical questions, which are written by Fabrizio Montanari. For instance, there is a long one about the Sacco-Vanzetti case that includes Turati's protests against their intended execution. Montanari's June 6, 2020, entry is entitled "*Mussolini e Treves: il duello alla Sciabola.*" It describes at length the Mussolini-Treves duel. The quote from the telegram Modigliani sent to Treves, *"I disapprove, I would have done the same, I salute you,"* is from this article.

The story of the duel is also recounted in Chapter VI of Steven C. Hughes' 2007 *Politics of the Sword: Dueling, Honor, and Masculinity in Modern Italy*, Ohio State University Press, Columbus.

24: The Great War

Denis Mack Smith's 1997 *Modern Italy: A Political History*, University of Michigan Press, Ann Arbor is an excellent source for this period of Italy's history. Chapter 7, pp. 271-276 describes Italy's conduct during the war, including the battle of Caporetto, and Chapter 38, pp. 276-282 describes the 1918-1920 Peace Conference that followed the war.

Some stories and statistics about Italian Jews fighting in WWI appear in pp.39-42 of Shira Klein's 2018 *Italy's Jews from Emancipation to Fascism*, Cambridge University Press, New York.

Pierluigi Briganti's 2009 *Il contributo militare degli ebrei italiani alla grande guerra (1915-1918)*, Zamorani, Turin is also helpful.

Ernest Hemingway. 1929. *A Farewell to Arms.* Scribner, New York. This novel, Hemingway's first great success, is about an American soldier who serves as a lieutenant in the ambulance corps of the Italian Army during WWI.

25: The War's Aftermath

The story of Italy between the end of WWI and the March on Rome that led to Mussolini's takeover of the Italian Government is well described in pp. 280-322 of Denis Mack Smith's 1997 *Modern Italy: A Political History,* University of Michigan Press, Ann Arbor.

The same delicate period is also described in Roberto Vivarelli's 1991 *Storia delle Origini del Fascismo: L'Italia dalla grande guerra alla marcia su Roma,* Volume 1, Il Mulino, Bologna.

The writings of Antonio Gramsci, imprisoned by the Fascists, have been recognized as important critiques of capitalist society. They can be found in John Cammett's 1967 *Antonio Gramsci and the Origins of Italian Communism,* Stanford University Press, Stanford.

26 The Rise of Fascism

Emilio Lussu. 1976. *Marcia su Roma e dintorni.* Einaudi, Turin. This book narrates the particulars of the March on Rome.

Details about the march can also be found in Chapter 5 of a book written by my cousin Claudio Gino Segrè (I am Gino Claudio). It is a biography of Italo Balbo, one of the four organizers of the march and later a prominent Fascist leader. Claudio Segrè.1987. *Italo Balbo: A Fascist Life.* University of California Press, Berkeley.

Renzo De Felice is widely considered the leading historian of Italy in the Fascist period, largely because of his six thousand (actually 6,284) page biography of Mussolini, *Mussolini.* Written between 1956 and 1996, it was published in four large volumes by Turin's Einaudi publishing house, the first volume appearing in 1965. Each volume contains two books that describe a phase of Mussolini's life, such as *Mussolini, il Rivoluzionario 1883-1920, Mussolini il fascista,* or *Mussolini il Duce,* etc. However, De Felice is considered by some to be too lenient in his condemnation of Mussolini. The controversies are explored at length by the historian Emilio Gentile in his biography of De Felice in the Diz. Bi.It. See also Shira Klein pp. 3-4.

De Felice, himself a Jew, also wrote a book about Italian Jews under Fascism that has been translated into English:

Renzo De Felice. 2001. *The Jews in Fascist Italy: A History.* Translated by Robert L. Miller. Enigma Books, New York.

One should also consult Michele Sarfatti, 2006, *The Jews in Mussolini's Italy: From Equality to Persecution*, University of Wisconsin Press, Madison.

Giacomo Matteotti's writings, which presumably led at least in part to his assassination, were published in England as Giacomo Matteotti's 1924 *The Fascisti Exposed: A Year of Fascist Domination,* translated by E. W. Dickes, Independent Labor Party Publication Dept., London

"*I shall give it all of these, if possible, with love but, if necessary, by force....*" This quote, widely considered to be the turning point in Mussolini's transition to a dictatorship, was delivered to the Chamber of Deputies on January 3, 1925. The full text can be found in Benito Mussolini's 1934 *Scritti e Discorsi, vol. 5, scritti e discorsi 1925 al 1926,*Ulrico Hoepli, Milan. It is also widely available online.

The rise of Fascism is also described in Section X of Denis Mack Smith's 1997 *Modern Italy: A Political History,* University of Michigan Press, Ann Arbor.

27: Turati's Escape

Giovanna Amato wrote the biography of Amelia Pincherle Rosselli in Diz.Bi.It,.

Amelia Rosselli's last book, *Fratelli Minori,* was reissued by Forgotten Books, London, in 2018.

Aldo Rosselli, son of Nello Rosselli, is a prolific author. One of his books is a family history that begins with his grandparents:

Aldo Rosselli. 2014. *La Famiglia Rosselli: Una Tragedia Italiana.* Castelvecchi, Rome.

Giuseppe Fiori's 1999 *Casa Rosselli: Vita di Carlo e Nello, Amelia, Marion e Maria,* Einaudi, Turin is another biography of the Rosselli family.

Stanislao Pugliese's 1999 *Carlo Rosselli, Socialist Heretic and Antifascist Exile,* Harvard University Press, Cambridge is an excellent biography in English of Carlo Rosselli.

The quote *"A Rosselli secretly sheltered a dying Mazzini...."* is from p.88 of this book.

For a collection of Carlo Rosselli's writings, see the 1996 edition of Roselli's *Liberal Socialism,* edited by Natia Urbinati, translated by William McCuaig, Princeton University Press, Princeton. One can only imagine what a political career Carlo Rosselli would have had in post-war Italy if he had not been assassinated.

Turati's week-long stay in medical researcher Giuseppe Levi's house is described by Levi's daughter Natalia (in her view of it as a teenager) in her marvelous book:

Natalia Ginzburg. 1984. *Family Sayings.* Translated by D. M. Low. Carcanet, Manchester.

28: Paris and Turin

Stanislao Pugliese. 1997. "Death in Exile: The Assassination of Carlo Rosselli." *Journal of Contemporary History.* Vol. 32 (3), 305–319.

Carlo Levi and Leone Ginzburg, both Turinese, were the Italian heads of Giustizià e Libertà. They were arrested and sent to a confino.

Carlo Levi, Claudio Treves' nephew, though trained as a doctor, wrote an important book after the war about his time in the confino. It went on to become an international best-seller that has been reissued as Carlo Levi's 2006 *Christ Stopped at Eboli: The Story of a Year,* translated by Frances Frenaye, Farrar, Straus & Giroux, New York.

Leone Ginzburg, a prominent anti-Fascist, was married to the novelist Natalia Ginzburg. Their time in the confino is described in her book *Family Sayings.* They are also the parents of the noted historian Carlo Ginzburg. Leone Ginzburg was captured by the Nazis and executed in February of 1944.

The quote from Turin's Rabbi Gino Bolaffio is from p. 53 of Alexander Stille's 1991 *Benevolence and Betrayal: Five Italian Jewish Families Under Fascism,* Summit Books, New York.

This book also describes how Ettore Ovazza, Fascist until the end, refused to leave Italy when his siblings did. He, his wife, and his daughter were killed by the Nazis in October of 1943.

29: The Racial Laws

The events of 1938 are treated in many of the books we have already referred to, such as:
Chapter XI, pp.426-529, of Riccardo Calimani's 2013 *Storia degli Ebrei Italiani: Nel XIX e nel XX secolo,* Mondadori, Milan.The chapter is appropriately entitled "1938: *L'Annus Horribils degli Ebrei Italiani.*"

See also:

Klein, *Italy's Jews from Emancipation to Fascism,* pp. 86-96
Attilio Milano 1963, pp. 396-400
Michele Sarfatti, *The Jews in Mussolini's Italy: From Equality to Persecution.*
Michele Sarfatti. 1994. *Mussolini contro gli ebrei. Cronaca dell'elaborazione delle leggi del 1938.* Zamorani, Turin.
Renzo De Felice, *The Jews in Fascist Italy: A History.*

Giorgio Bassani's 1977 *The Garden of the Finzi-Continis,* Harcourt, Brace and Jovanovich, Boston,is a novelistic account of the times, and Alexander Stille's *Benevolence and Betrayal: Five Jewish Families under Fascism* provides some detailed case studies of families dealing with the Racial Laws.

30: The Boys of Via Panisperna

Edoardo Amaldi. 1997. *Da via Panisperna all'America.* Edited by Giovanni Battimelli and Michelangelo de Maria. Editori Riuniti, Rome.

Frank Close. 2015. *Half-Life: The Divided Life of Bruno Pontecorvo, Physicist or Spy.* Basic Books, New York.

Valeria del Gamba. 2007. *Il Ragazzo di Via Panisperna: L'Avventurosa Vita del fisico Franco Rasetti.* Bollati Boringhieri, Turin.

Laura Fermi. 1954. *Atoms in the Family: My Life with Enrico Fermi.* University of Chicago Press, Chicago.

Salvador Luria. 1984. *A Slot Machine, a Broken Test Tube: An Autobiography.* Harpercollins, New York.

Gino Segrè and Bettina Hoerlin. 2016. *The Pope of Physics: Enrico Fermi and the Birth of the Atomic Age.* Henry Holt, New York.

Emilio Segrè. 1999. *A Mind Always in Motion: The Autobiography of Emilio Segrè.* University of California Press, Berkeley.

"His methods were always simple. . . ." is a quote from p.86 of Rudolf Peierls' 1985 *Bird of Passage: Recollections of a Physicist,* Princeton University Press, Princeton.

Works Cited

Alighieri, Dante. *La Divina Commedia.* 1933. Edited by C. H. Grandgent. D.C. Heath &Co., Boston.

Amaldi, Edoardo. 1997. *Da via Panisperna all'America.* Edited by Giovanni Battimelli and Michelangelo de Maria. Editori Riuniti, Rome.

Babbitt, Donald and Judith Goodstein. "Federigo Enriques's Quest to Prove the 'Completeness Theorem'." *Notices of the American Mathematical Society* 58: 240-249.

Ballini, Pier Luigi, ed. 2000. *Sidney Sonnino e il suo Tempo.* Leo Olschki, Florence.

Bassani, Giorgio. 1977. *The Garden of the Finzi-Continis,* Harcourt, Brace and Jovanovich, Boston,

Beales, Derick and Eugenio Biagini. 2003. *The Risorgimento and the Unification of Italy.* Routledge, London.

Berger, David. 1979. "*Cum Nimis Absurdum* and the Conversion of the Jews." Jewish Quarterly Review. New Series. 70 (1): 41–49.

Bettoni, Ludovico and Claudio Segrè. 2000. *Dall'Ancien Regime all' Età Borghese: Bozzolo, la Comunità Ebraica e le sue famiglie (1597-1955).* Grafo, Brescia.

Briano, Italo. 1977. *Storia delle ferrovie in Italia.* Cavallotti Editore, Milan.

Briganti, Pierluigi. 2009. *Il contributo militare degli ebrei italiani alla grande guerra (1915-1918).* Zamorani, Turin.

Buseghin, Maria Luciana. 2022. "Alice Hallgarten Franchetti: A Woman Beyond Barriers," in *A Female Activist Elite in Italy (1890–1920).* Edited by Elena Laurenzi and Manuela Mosca. Springer Professional, New York.

Calimani, Riccardo. 1987. *The Ghetto of Venice.* Translated by Katherine Silberblatt Wolfthal. M. Evans & Co., New York.

Calimani, Riccardo. 2013. *Storia degli Ebrei Italiani: Nel XIX e nel XX secolo.* Mondadori, Milan.

Calimani, Riccardo. 2016. *Storia degli Ebrei Italiani: Dalle Origini al XV secolo.* Mondadori, Milan.

Cammett, John. 1967. *Antonio Gramsci and the Origins of Italian Communism.* Stanford University Press, Stanford.

Casalini, Maria. 1987. *La signora del socialismo italiano: Vita di Anna Kuliscioff.* Editori Riuniti, Rome

Castelnuovo, Enrico. 2017. *The Moncalvos.* Translated by Brenda Webster and Gabriella Romani. Wings Press, San Antonio

Ciani, Nadia. 2007. *Da Mazzini al Campidoglio: Vita di Ernesto Nathan.* Ediesse, Rome.

Close, Frank. 2015. *Half-Life: The Divided Life of Bruno Pontecorvo, Physicist or Spy.* Basic Books, New York.

Coppa, Frank J. 2003. "Pio Nono and the Jews: from 'Reform' to 'Reaction,' 1846 to 1878," *The Catholic Historical Review,* Vol. 89, No. 4. Catholic University of America Press, Washington D.C.

Damiani, Franco and Fabio Rodriguez. 1978. *Anna Kuliscioff: Immagini, scritti, testimonianze.* Feltrinelli Economica, Milan.

De Felice, Renzo. 1965-1997. *Mussolini, 4 volumes.* Einaudi, Turin.

De Felice, Renzo. 2001. *The Jews in Fascist Italy: A History.* Translated by Robert L. Miller. Enigma Books, New York.

Del Canuto, Francesco. 1972. *Il Movimento sionistico in Italia dalle origini al 1924.* Federazione Sionistica Italiana, Milano.

del Gamba, Valeria. 2007. *Il Ragazzo di Via Panisperna: L'Avventurosa Vita del fisico Franco Rasetti.* Bollati Boringhieri, Turin.

Di Scala, Spencer. 1980. *Dilemmas of Italian Socialism: The Politics of Filippo Turati.* University of Massachusetts Press, Amherst.

Dizionario Biografico degli Italiani. Istituto dell'Enciclopedia Italiana, Rome. https://www.treccani.it/biografico/

Fargion, Liliana Picciotto. 1991. *Il Libro della Memoria: Gli Ebrei Deportati dall'Italia (1943-1945).* Mursia, Milan.

Fargion, Liliana Pocciotto. 1979. "*Testimonianza di un deportato da Roma,*" in *L'occupazione tedesca e gli ebrei di Roma: Documenti e fatti.* Carucci, Rome

Fazio, Vero. 2021. *Il Seguito della Storia: Giacomo e Roberto Segre tra Breccia di Porta Pia e Grande Guerra. Belforte, Livorno*

Fermi, Laura. 1954. *Atoms in the Family: My Life with Enrico Fermi.* University of Chicago Press, Chicago.

Finzi, Ermanno. 2017. *E alla Fine Non Rimase Nessuno.* Istituto Mantovano di Storia Contemporanea, Mantua

Fiorentino, Luca and Annie Sacerdoti. 1989. *Guide to Jewish Italy.* Israelowitz, Brooklyn.

Fiori, Giuseppe. 1999. *Casa Rosselli: Vita di Carlo e Nello, Amelia, Marion e Maria.* Einaudi, Turin

Ford, Kenneth and John Archibald Wheeler. 2000. *Geons, Black Holes and Quantum Foam: A Life in Physics.* W.W. Norton &Co., New York

Franchetti, Leopoldo and Sidney Sonnino. 1925. *La Sicilia nel 1876.* Vallecchi, Florence.

Genovesi, Giovanni. 2010. *Storia della scuola in Italia dal Settecento a oggi.* Laterza, Bari.

Ginzburg, Natalia. 1984. *Family Sayings.* Translated by D. M. Low. Carcanet, Manchester.

Giolitti, Giovanni. 1982. *Memorie della mia Vita.* Garzanti, Milan.

Goodstein, Judith. 2007. *The Volterra Chronicles: The life and Times of an Extraordinary Mathematician: 1860-1940.* American Mathematical Society, Providence, RI.

Goodstein, Judith. 2010. *Einstein's Italian Mathematicians: Ricci, Levi-Civita, and the Birth of General Relativity.* American Mathematical Society, Providence, RI.

Gregorovius, Ferdinand. 1948. *Ghetto and the Jews of Rome.* Translated by Moses Hadas. Schocken Books, New York.

Hemingway, Ernest. 1929. *A Farewell to Arms.* Scribner, New York.

Heyries, Hubert. 2020. *La Breccia di Porta Pia:20 Settembre 1870.* Il Mulino, Bologna.

Hughes, Steven C. 2007. *Politics of the Sword: Dueling, Honor, and Masculinity in Modern Italy.* Ohio State University Press, Columbus.

Hughes, Stuart H. 1983. *Prisoners of Hope: The Silver Age of the Italian Jews 1924-1974.* Harvard University Press, Cambridge, Mass

Italy's National Statistics Bureau, ISTAT. Istituto Nazionale di Statistica, Rome. https://www.istat.it.

Kertzer, David. 1997. *The Kidnapping of Edgardo Mortara.* Vintage Books, New York.

Kertzer, David. 2004. *Prisoner of the Vatican.* Houghton Mifflin, Boston.

Klein, Shira. 2018. *Italy's Jews from Emancipation to Fascism.* Cambridge University Press, New York.

Kuliscioff, Anna. 2021. *The Monopoly of Man.* Translated by Lorenzo Chiesa. MIT Press, Cambridge.

Lattes, Dante. 1928. *Il Sionismo.* Cremonese, Rome.

Levi, Carlo. 2006. Christ Stopped at Eboli: The Story of a Year. Translated by Frances Frenaye. Farrar, Straus & Giroux, New York.

Levi, Primo. 1961. *Survival in Auschwitz.* Translated by Stuart Woolf. Collier Books, New York.

Luria, Salvador. 1984. *A Slot Machine, a Broken Test Tube: An Autobiography*. Harper Collins, New York.

Lussu, Emilio. 1976. *Marcia su Roma e dintorni.* Einaudi, Turin.

Luzzatti, Luigi. 1935. *Memorie Tratte dal Carteggio.* Zanichelli, Bologna

Luzzatti, Luigi. 2005. *God in Freedom: Studies in the Relations Between Church and State.* Translated by Alfonso Arbib-Costa. Cosimo Classics, New York.

Macioti, Maria Immacolata. 2021. *Nathan: Il sindaco di Roma dalla parte del popolo.* Newton, Rome.

Mack Smith, Denis. 1997. *Modern Italy: A Political History.* University of Michigan Press, Ann Arbor.

Manzoni, Alessandro. 2022. *The Betrothed* (1827). Translated by Michael F. Moore. Modern Library Classics, New York.

Martini, Fabio. 2007. *Nathan e l'invenzione di Roma: Il sindaco che cambiò la Città eterna.* Marsilio, Venice.

Massari, Giuseppe. 1880. *Il Generale Alfonso La Marmora.* Barbèra, Florence.

Matteotti, Giacomo. 1924. *The Fascisti Exposed: A Year of Fascist Domination.* Translated by E. W. Dickes. Independent Labor Party Publication Dept., London

Mazzini, Giuseppe. 1862. *The Duties of Man.* Chapman & Hall, London.

Milano, Attilio. 1963. *Storia degli Ebrei in Italia.* Einaudi, Turin.

Momigliano, Arnaldo. 1985. "The Jews of Italy." *The New York Review of Books.* October 24, 1985. https://www.nybooks.com/articles/1985/10/24/the-jews-of-italy/

Montanari, Fabrizio. 2020. "Mussolini e Treves: il duello alla Sciabola." *24 Emilia.* June 6, 2020. https://www.24emilia.com/mussolini-e-treves-il-duello-alla-sciabola/

Mussolini, Benito. 1934. *Scritti e Discorsi, vol. 5, scritti e discorsi 1925 al 1926.* Ulrico Hoepli, Milan.

Pavan, Ilaria. 2006. *Il podesta` ebreo: La storia di Renzo Ravenna tra fascismo e leggi razziali.* Laterza, Bari.

Peierls, Rudolf. 1985. *Bird of Passage: Recollections of a Physicist.* Princeton University Press, Princeton.

Pugliese, Stanislao. 1997. "Death in Exile: The Assassination of Carlo Rosselli." Journal of Contemporary History. Vol. 32 (3), 305–319.

Pugliese, Stanislao. 1999. *Carlo Rosselli, Socialist Heretic and Antifascist Exile.* Harvard University Press, Cambridge.

Riall, Lucy. 1994. *The Italian Risorgimento: State, Society and National Unification.* Routledge, London.

Riall, Lucy. 2009. *Risorgimento: The History of Italy from Napoleon to Nation State.* Palgrave Macmillan, London.

Roselli, Carlo. 2017. *Liberal Socialism.* Edited by Natia Urbinati, translated by William McCuaig. Princeton University Press, Princeton

Rosselli, Aldo. 2014. *La Famiglia Rosselli: Una Tragedia Italiana.* Castelvecchi, Rome.

Rosselli, Amelia. 2018. *Fratelli Minori.* Forgotten Books, London.

Roth, Cecil. 1946. *The History of the Jews of Italy.* Jewish Publication Society of America, Philadelphia,

Sarfatti, Michele. 1994. *Mussolini contro gli ebrei. Cronaca dell'elaborazione delle leggi del 1938.* Zamorani, Turin.

Sarfatti, Michele. 2006. *The Jews in Mussolini's Italy: From Equality to Persecution.* Translated by John and Anne C. Tedeschi. University of Wisconsin Press, Madison.

Schächter, Elizabeth. 2011. *The Jews of Italy, 1848-1915: Between Tradition and Transformation.* Vallentine Mitchell, London

Segre, Augusto. 1979. *Memorie di Vita Ebraica: Casale Monferrato, Roma Gerusalemme, 1918-1960.* Bonacci, Rome.

Segrè, Claudio. 1987. *Italo Balbo: A Fascist Life.* University of California Press, Berkeley.

Segrè, Emilio. 1999. *A Mind Always in Motion: The Autobiography of Emilio Segrè.* University of California Press, Berkeley.

Segrè, Gino and Bettina Hoerlin. 2016. *The Pope of Physics: Enrico Fermi and the Birth of the Atomic Age.* Henry Holt, New York.

Sereni, Emilio. 1997. *History of the Italian Agricultural Scene,* Princeton University Press, Princeton.

Stille, Alexander. 1991. *Benevolence and Betrayal: Five Italian Jewish Families Under Fascism.* Summit Books, New York

Suetonius. 2007. *The Twelve Caesars.* Translated by Robert Graves. Penguin Classics, London.

Toscano, Mario. 2019. *Ebrei e Ebraismo nell'Italia del Novecento.* Franco Angeli, Rome.

Treves Levi Vidale, Silvia. 1990. *All'Ombra Degli Avi* (*In the Shade of the Ancestors*). Unpublished memoir.

Ugolini, Romano. 2003. *Ernesto Nathan tra idealità e pragmatismo.* Edizioni dell'Ateneo, Rome.

Vivarelli, Roberto. 1991. *Storia delle Origini del Fascismo: L'Italia dalla grande guerra alla marcia su Roma.* Il Mulino, Bologna.

Zuccotti, Susan. 1987. *The Italians and the Holocaust: Persecution, Rescue, and Survival.* Basic Books, New York.

Gino Segrè has authored five books on the history of science: *A Matter of Degrees* (2002), *Faust in Copenhagen* (2007), *Ordinary Geniuses* (2011), *The Pope of Physics* (2016) with Bettina Hoerlin, and *Unearthing Fermi's Geophysics* (2021) with John Stack. *The Pope of Physics* was a *New York Times Book Review* Editor's Choice and named a Best Book of the Year by *Bloomberg*; *Faust in Copenhagen* was a finalist for the *LA Times* Book Prize. Segrè was born in Florence, Italy and raised there and in New York City. He is a former chair and professor emeritus of physics and astronomy at the University of Pennsylvania and has received awards from the National Science Foundation, the U.S. Department of Energy, the Alfred P. Sloan Foundation, and the John Simon Guggenheim Memorial Foundation. He lives in Philadelphia with his wife Bettina Hoerlin.